Paper Bag Puppets

SCHOOL LIBRARY MEDIA SERIES

Edited by Diane de Cordova Biesel

1. *Chalk Talk Stories*, written and illustrated by Arden Druce, 1993.
2. *Toddler Storytime Programs*, by Diane Briggs, 1993.
3. *Alphabet: A Handbook of ABC Books and Book Extensions for the Elementary Classroom, second edition*, by Patricia L. Roberts, 1994.
4. *Cultural Cobblestones: Teaching Cultural Diversity*, by Lynda Miller, Theresa Steinlage, and Mike Printz, 1994.
5. *ABC Books and Activities: From Preschool to High School*, by Cathie Hilterbran Cooper, 1996.
6. *ZOOLUTIONS: A Mathematical Expedition with Topics for Grades 4 through 8*, by Anne Burgunder and Vaunda Nelson, 1996.
7. *Library Lessons for Grades 7–9*, by Arden Druce, 1997.
8. *Counting Your Way through 1–2–3 Books and Activities*, by Cathie Hilterbran Cooper, 1997.
9. *Art and Children: Using Literature to Expand Creativity*, by Robin W. Davis, 1996.
10. *Story Programs: A Source Book of Materials, second edition*, by Carolyn Sue Peterson and Ann Fenton, 1998.
11. *Taking Humor Seriously in Children's Literature: Literature-Based Mini-Units and Humorous Books for Children Ages 5–12*, by Patricia L. Roberts, 1997.
12. *Multicultural Friendship Stories and Activities for Children, Ages 5–14*, by Patricia L. Roberts, 1997.
13. *Side by Side: Twelve Multicultural Puppet Plays*, by Jean M. Pollock, 1997.
14. *Reading Fun: Quick and Easy Activities for the School Library Media Center*, by Mona Kerby, 1997.
15. *Paper Bag Puppets*, by Arden Druce with illustrations by Geraldine Hulbert, Cynthia Johnson, Harvey H. Lively, and Carol Ditter Waters, 1999.
16. *Once Upon a Childhood: Fingerplays, Action Rhymes, and Fun Times for the Very Young*, by Dolores C. Chupela, 1998.
17. *Bulletin Bored? or Bulletin Boards!: K–12*, by Patricia Sivak and Mary Anne Passatore, 1998.
18. *Color and Shape Books for All Ages*, by Cathie Hilterbran Cooper, 1998.

Paper Bag Puppets

Arden Druce

Illustrated by Geraldine Hulbert, Cynthia Johnson,
Harvey H. Lively, Carol Ditter Waters

School Library Media Series,
No. 15

The Scarecrow Press, Inc.
Lanham, MD & London
1999

SCARECROW PRESS, INC.

Published in the United States of America
by Scarecrow Press, Inc.
4720 Boston Way, Lanham, Maryland 20706
http://www.scarecrowpress.com

4 Pleydell Gardens, Folkestone
Kent CT20 2DN, England

British Library Cataloguing in Publication Information Available

Library of Congress Cataloging-in-Publication Data

Druce, Arden.
    Paper bag puppets / Arden Druce : illustrated by Geraldine
Hulbert . . . [et al.].
    p. cm. — (School library media series ; no. 15)
    Includes index.
    ISBN 0-8108-3400-6 (paper : alk. paper)
    1. Children's libraries—Activity programs—United States. 2. Storytelling—United
States. 3. Libraries and puppets—United States. 4. Puppet theater in education—United
States. 5. Teaching—United States—Aids and devices. 6. Biography—Study and
teaching. 7. United States—Biography—Study and teaching. I. Title. II. Series.
   2718.3 .D78 1999
   027.62'51—dc21   97-37705
                                                   CIP

Contents

Series Editor's Foreword

The School Library Media series is directed to the school library media specialist, particularly the building level librarian. The multifaceted role of the librarian as educator, collection developer, curriculum developer, and information specialist is examined. The series includes concise, practical books on topical and current subjects related to programs and services.

In her third book for Scarecrow Press, Arden Druce has designed patterns and a script for over 100 puppets. Basic biographical information in the form of riddles is provided for each character. With inexpensive supplies (paper bags and glue), teachers and librarians can direct students of varying ages to make these simple puppets to enhance social studies, literary, and holiday activities.

Diane de Cordova Biesel
Series Editor

Introduction

Paper Bag Puppets was created for the use of librarians, teachers, and students. Most of the chapters have three parts: suggestions for the use of its puppets, the puppet patterns, and biographical riddles or stories about the puppets.

Because seven of the eight chapters were originally individual books, there are a few duplications. For example, portraits of Abraham Lincoln are found in two chapters and are illustrated by two different illustrators. To give the reader an alternative choice in selecting a portrait, both renderings have been included.

Besides using the table of contents to locate a particular group of portraits, the reader can use the index in some instances. For example, to locate portraits for Black History Month, refer to African Americans in the index. To locate portraits of presidents, some of which are not in the Famous Presidents chapter, refer to the index under Presidents.

Puppets are fun. Enjoy them and let your students enjoy them, too.

Construction and Manipulation

Foundation

Use brown or white paper bags, preferably size 5-1/8" x 3-1/8" x 10-5/8". Although the puppets were designed to fit the size recommended, different size bags may be used. If using a different size bag, determine where the puppet's two parts need to be placed to achieve a perfect fit before applying paste.

Paper for the Puppets

Use typing paper, tag board, poster board, or construction paper. White is best for Caucasians. Brown is effective for Native Americans and African Americans.

Making and Reproducing a Pattern

To make a pattern, photocopy the puppet. To reproduce multiple copies on typing paper, photocopy or make a spirit master on a thermo copier and then put the master on a duplicator. To make multiple copies on tag board, poster board, or construction paper, use the pattern to make a spirit master on a thermo copier and then put the master on a duplicator.

Coloring the Puppet

It is not necessary to color the puppet. However, if desired the eyes, brows, hair, and clothes may be colored. African Americans and Native Americans made from rich brown construction paper are effective with black eyes, brows, and hair.

Cutting

Cut the puppet out.

Pasting

Check to determine if the fit is perfect before pasting. Place the lower part of the face up to the crease under the flap. Place the upper part of the face on the flap, ending at the lower edge. If the recommended size bag is being used, there should be a perfect fit. If using a different size bag, move the two parts on the bag until a fit is achieved. If desired, designate the locations with a pencil.

Paste the lower part of the face first. If this part does not extend past the bag, apply the paste to the puppet part and affix. If the lower part extends past the bag's sides (particularly found among Storybook and Halloween puppets), apply the paste to the bag, but NOT TO THE PUPPET, to prevent the extended area from sticking to the table, etc. If students are making puppets, direct them explicitly on this point.

After checking the position of the upper part of the face, apply paste to the top of the flap, NOT TO THE PUPPET. This will prevent paste from extending past the bag and adhering to the table, etc. Affix the upper part of the face to the bag.

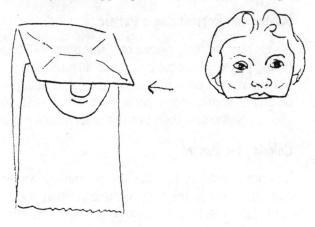

Identifying

If students are making puppets, have them write their names and the names of their puppets on the back side of their paper bags.

Manipulation

Put your hand into the paper bag, with the fingers fitting down into the flap. Move the fingers toward and away from the palm to give the puppet the appearance of talking.

I
Famous Americans

Illustrated by
Geraldine Hulbert

Use of the Puppets

Teacher/Librarian Use

Some ways to use the puppets in the Famous Americans chapter are as follows:

1. To introduce a unit, story, research, or biography
2. To review famous Americans covered in the social studies or English curriculum
3. To culminate a unit in which famous Americans figure prominently
4. To feature a famous American in relation to a specific event
   - Columbus Day—In celebration of Columbus Day, present the Columbus puppet and riddle. If desired, have students make Columbus puppets.
   - Abraham Lincoln's Birthday—Present the Abraham Lincoln puppet and riddle. If desired, have students make Abraham Lincoln puppets.
   - George Washington's Birthday—Present the George Washington puppet and riddle. If desired, have students make George Washington puppets.
   - Fourth of July—Present the Uncle Sam puppet. If desired, have students make Uncle Sam puppets.
5. To enrich a bulletin board display of student reports or a display of book jackets about famous Americans

Student Use

Students may research, make, and present the puppets.

Recreational Use

The puppets may be used in recreational settings, such as at camp, at home, etc.

Christopher Columbus

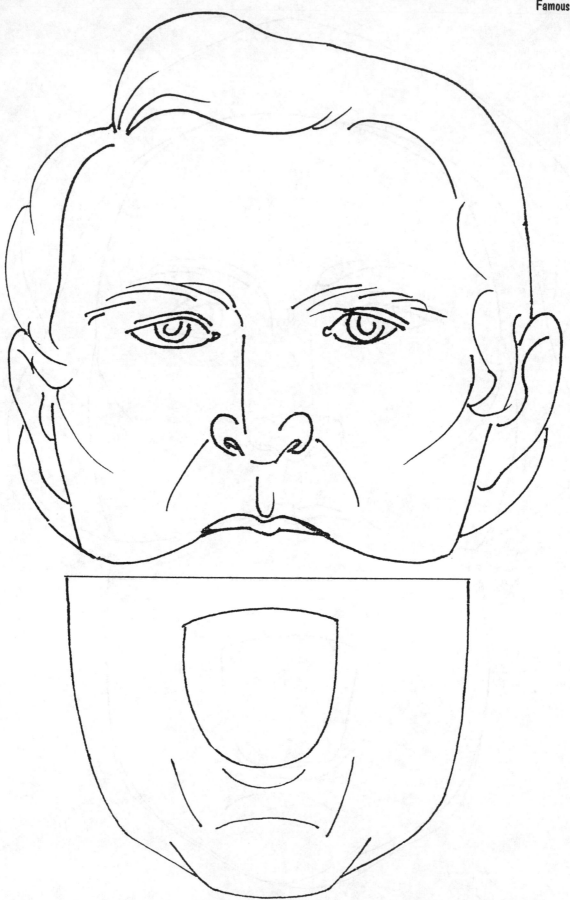

John Adams

Ethan Allen

Clara Barton

Alexander Graham Bell

Daniel Boone

Henry Clay

Davy Crockett

George Custer

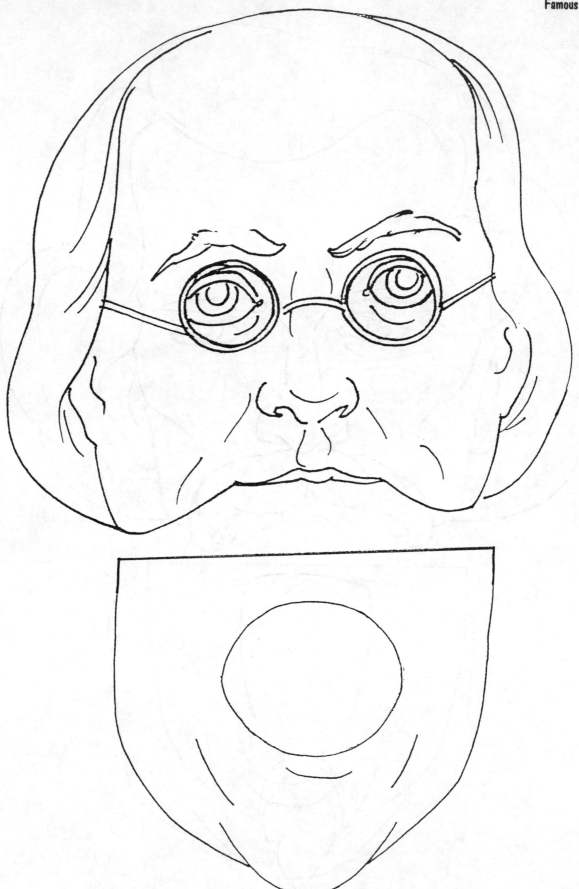

Benjamin Franklin

Robert Fulton

Ulysses S. Grant

Alexander Hamilton

John Hancock

Patrick Henry

Andrew Jackson

Thomas Jefferson

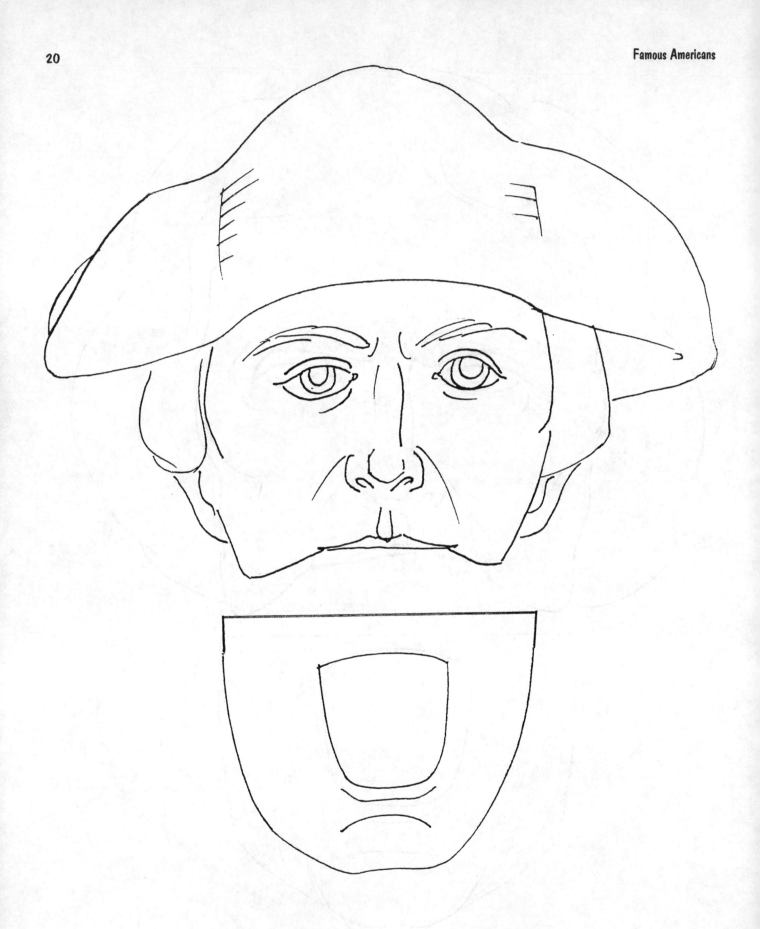

John Paul Jones

Robert E. Lee

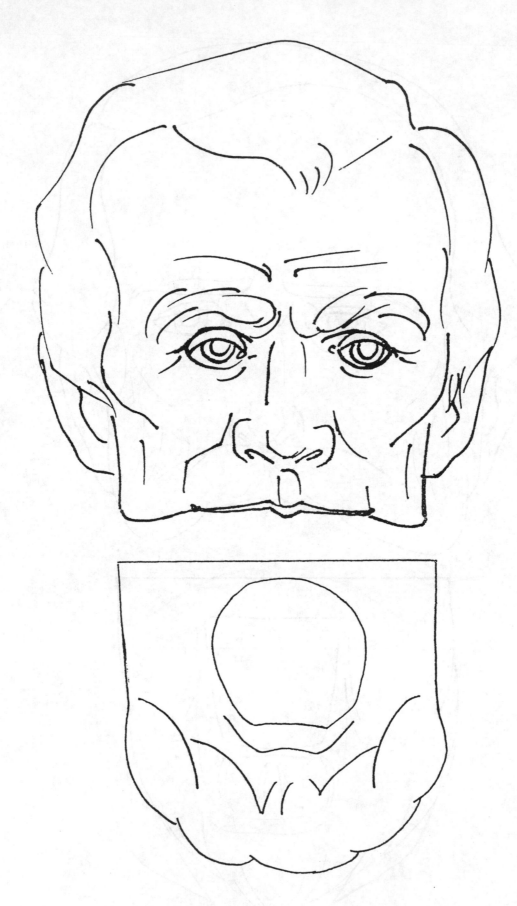

Abraham Lincoln

Tom Paine

Pocahontas

Paul Revere

Theodore Roosevelt

Betsy Ross

Sacajawea

Uncle Sam (Part 1)

Uncle Sam (Part 2)

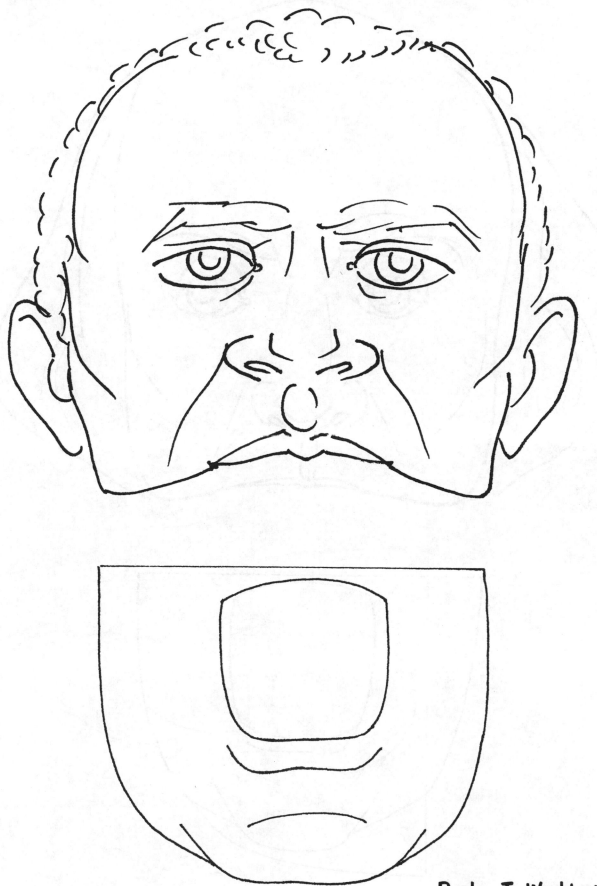

Booker T. Washington

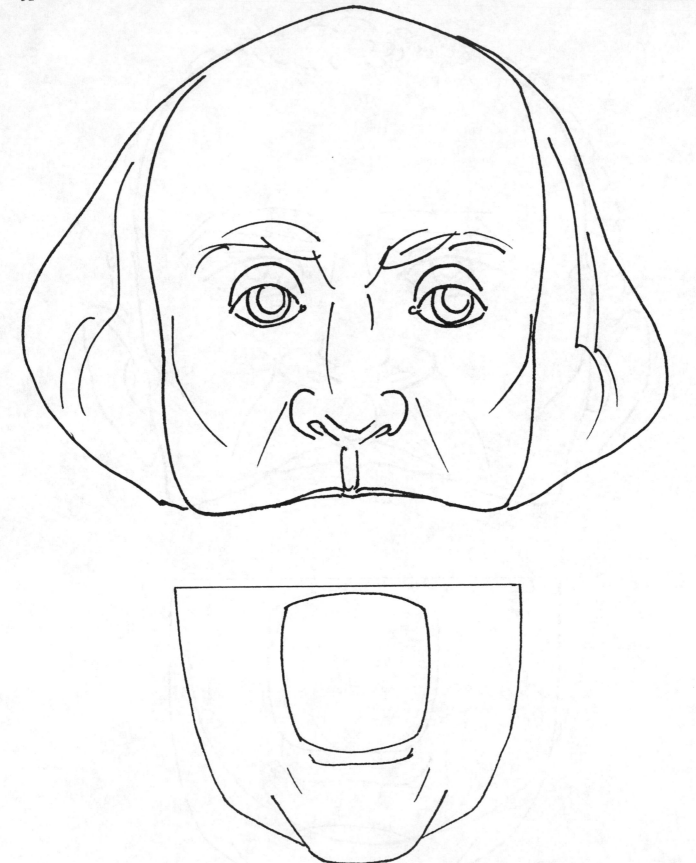

George Washington

Daniel Webster

Riddles to Use with the Puppets

These riddles, which provide basic biographical information, may be told by either the instructor or by the students. If students are presenting the puppets, the instructor may let the students use the riddles in this book or may choose to have students do research and make up their own riddles. In a presentation, the puppet's name is withheld. The puppeteer tells a riddle and at the conclusion chooses a student to identify the puppet.

CHRISTOPHER COLUMBUS (1451-1506)

I was born in Italy in 1451.

When I was young most people believed that the earth was flat. They believed that strange monsters and dragons lived in the sea. I believed the earth was round. I believed that if I sailed west, I would come to the East.

When I grew up, King Ferdinand and Queen Isabella of Spain helped me to get three ships to sail across the ocean. On October 12, 1492, my ship reached land. I thought I had arrived in the Indies, so I called the people I saw Indians. I had actually found a new world. I had found America.

Who was I?

JOHN ADAMS (1735-1826)

I was born in Massachusetts in 1735. As a youth I was trained to uphold high standards. I was honest, thrifty, religious, and obedient to my parents. I took the responsibility that went with wealth and education seriously.

Before I was twenty I graduated from college. I became a teacher, a lawyer, and a member of the Continental Congress. I eventually became the first Vice President of the United States. In 1796, I became the second President of the United States. Avoiding war with France was one of my major accomplishments.

I lived to see my son become the sixth President of the United States. When asked to give a toast for a Fourth of July celebration, I replied: "Independence Forever!"

Who was I?

ETHAN ALLEN (1738-1789)

I was born in Connecticut in 1738. Years later I served in the French and Indian War and then settled in Vermont.

When the British decided that New York owned the land that had been granted to the settlers and ruled that the settlers must buy their land a second time, Seth Warner and I organized the Green Mountain Boys. As a group, we not only fought off settlers from New York but also fought the officials.

When the Revolutionary War broke out in 1775, the Green Mountain Boys joined with the patriot cause. We captured Fort Ticonderoga, which was one of the first important American victories of the Revolutionary War.

I was a patriot, a soldier, and the leader of the Green Mountain Boys.

Who was I?

CLARA BARTON (1821-1912)

I was born on Christmas Day, 1821, in Massachusetts. When I grew up, I went to Washington and took a government job. During the War Between the States, I helped find medicine, bandages, and food for the wounded soldiers who were brought to the city. When I learned that many soldiers had died because they had lain on the battlefields for hours or days before being brought to Washington, I decided to go to the battlefield to help them. For four years I followed the soldiers to battle.

After the war, when I was in Europe, I learned of the International Red Cross Committee. When I came home I started the American Red Cross. At the age of eighty-one I began to teach something that was an important new addition to the Red Cross: first-aid classes.

I was a nurse, a teacher, and the founder of the American Red Cross.

Who was I?

ALEXANDER GRAHAM BELL (1847-1922)

I was born in Scotland in 1847. When I grew up I became a teacher of the deaf. My method of teaching was so successful that I was invited to the United States. I moved to the United States, became an American citizen, and lived here the rest of my life.

Through teaching the deaf, I became interested in the sound of the human voice. I thought it might be possible to send sound across a distance. My assistant, Mr. Watson, and I worked day and night trying to invent a telephone. After failing many times, I finally said over the telephone from some distance, "Mr. Watson, please come here. I want you." That was the first telephone message ever sent.

I was a teacher of the deaf, and I invented the telephone.

Who was I?

DANIEL BOONE (1734-1820)

I was born in Pennsylvania in 1734. When I was a boy I studied every growing thing in the woods. I learned to imitate the call of birds. I could identify animals by the sounds they made.

When I grew up I fought many warlike Indian tribes. In one battle I was captured and held prisoner. The Indians liked me, and their chief wanted to adopt me as a son. Months passed before I was able to escape.

As new settlers began to move into the state where I lived, I became restless. I moved west where there were fewer people.

I was a pioneer, hunter, and explorer.
Who was I?

HENRY CLAY (1777-1852)

I was born in Virginia in 1777. I had little education, but I loved to read.

I became a lawyer and served in Congress as a representative and as a senator. I ran for president three times, but never won. I helped hold the Union together through compromises between the North and South and became known as "the Great Compromiser." John C. Calhoun, Daniel Webster, and I nearly controlled Congress for a number of years.

I am remembered for my remark, "I had rather be right than President." Another of my famous statements was "I know no North, no South, no East, no West."

I was a leading statesman for forty years.
Who was I?

DAVY CROCKETT (1786-1836)

I was born in 1786 in Tennessee. Years later I became a scout for Andrew Jackson and served in the Tennessee militia. I was a hunter and frontiersman. I wrote several humorous books about my life and adventures.

I served in Congress three terms. After I left Congress, I joined about 186 men in the Alamo, where we were besieged by 5,000 Mexicans. I died in the last assault, my body riddled with bullets. Every man in the Alamo was killed.

I was a famous frontiersman, scout, soldier, hunter, congressman, and humorist.
Who was I?

GEORGE CUSTER (1839-1876)

I was born in Ohio in 1839. During the Civil War, at the age of twenty-three, I became the youngest general in the Union Army. After the war, I was dropped to the rank of captain. On one occasion I was ordered to round up the Sioux and Cheyenne Indians and take them to reservations. There were many more Indians than I had thought. In the fight, called the battle of Little Big Horn, I was killed along with my column of about 225 men. Not a man survived. The battle is known as Custer's last stand. I was an American Army officer who won fame as an Indian fighter.
Who was I?

BENJAMIN FRANKLIN (1706-1790)

I was born in Massachusetts in 1706.

When I grew up, I published a newspaper. I also published *Poor Richard's Almanac,* which included a number of wise sayings, such as:

"If a thing is worth doing, it is worth doing well."

"Never leave that till tomorrow which you can do today."

"Early to bed and early to rise, makes a man healthy, wealthy, and wise."

I started the first public library and the first fire department in America, and I helped to start the first American police department. I invented an iron stove and bifocal glasses.

I was one of the signers of the Declaration of Independence, and I was a member of the Convention that wrote the Constitution of the United States.

I was a printer, a publisher, an inventor, and an American who served my country.

Who was I?

ROBERT FULTON (1765-1815)

I was born in 1765 on a farm in Pennsylvania. When I was very young, I showed a talent for invention. I made household utensils, lead pencils, and skyrockets. I developed a paddle wheel for a rowboat, and I constructed a rifle with original designs.

At seventeen I was apprenticed to a jeweler. I made a name for myself by painting miniatures and portraits. I bought a farm for my mother with money I saved. I studied art, but I became so interested in science and engineering that my art became only an amusement to me.

I am best remembered for building the steamboat, *Clermont*. It wasn't the first steamboat to be built, but it was the first to be practical and successful.

I was an American inventor, engineer, and artist.

Who was I?

ULYSSES S. GRANT (1822-1885)

I was born in Ohio in 1822.

I became an officer in the U.S. Army upon graduating from the U.S. Military Academy at West Point. I served in the Army during the war with Mexico. After eleven years in the Army, I left to become a farmer. I didn't do well as a farmer. I failed in real estate, too.

When the Civil War broke out, I returned to the Army, where I achieved one victory after another. Finally President Lincoln made me leader of all the Union's forces. I led the Union to victory again. General Robert E. Lee surrendered the war to me at Appomattox.

I was a hero to the people. They elected me president of the United States twice. I was a soldier, the leader of the Northern armies during the Civil War, and the eighteenth President of the United States.

Who was I?

ALEXANDER HAMILTON (1757-1804)

I was born in the West Indies in 1757. When I was eleven my mother died.

My father failed in business and it became necessary for me to make my own living. I went to work for a merchant, but I really wanted to be a writer. I wrote articles and sent them to newspapers. They were so well received that my friends and others raised enough money to send me to New York to study.

In America I became interested in the trouble between the American colonists and England. I made speeches and wrote articles saying the Americans were in the right. When George Washington was chosen President of the United States, I was selected to be secretary of the treasury.

I opposed Aaron Burr when he ran for President of the United States and when he ran for governor of New York. He later challenged me to a duel. I did not believe that duels were right, but I also did not believe I could refuse to fight. I was wounded seriously in the duel, and I died the next day. Many Americans mourned my death. I was a soldier, a leader, and a patriot.

Who was I?

JOHN HANCOCK (1737-1793)

I was born in Massachusetts in 1737. My father died when I was a boy, and my uncle adopted me. Later when my uncle died, I took over his business.

I was the first to sign the Declaration of Independence and am especially remembered for the great boldness with which I signed it.

On one occasion the British were going to arrest Samuel Adams and myself, but Paul Revere warned us, and we escaped.

I was a patriot who is well remembered.

Who was I?

PATRICK HENRY (1736-1799)

I was born in Virginia in 1736. When I grew up, I became a lawyer and soon won fame as an orator. I was a leader in Virginia and in the colonies. I was elected governor six times, but I accepted only five terms. I opposed the ratification of the United States Constitution. I believed the Constitution endangered the rights of the individual and the state. When I lost, I accepted the Constitution. I was largely responsible for the Bill of Rights.

I am best remembered for my words: "Give me liberty or give me death." I was a distinguished statesman and orator at the time of the Revolutionary War.

Who was I?

ANDREW JACKSON (1767-1845)

In 1767 I was born near the border between North and South Carolina. My father and mother died while I was young. Thereafter, I found work to support myself, and later I studied law and became a lawyer.

I moved to Tennessee, served actively in state and federal government, and became one of Tennessee's most important citizens. I won fame as an Indian fighter, and I served at the Battle of New Orleans.

In 1828 I was elected President of the United States. Because I was as strong in mind and body as hickory wood, I was called "Old Hickory." I spent my last years at my beautiful home, The Hermitage.

Who was I?

THOMAS JEFFERSON (1743-1826)

I was born in Virginia in 1743. My father, a pioneer, taught me never to ask another to do for me what I could do for myself. I learned to ride a horse, shoot a gun, paddle a canoe, and hunt.

I began studying when I was five years old, and I studied all my life. I played the violin. I was a farmer, surveyor, lawyer, and scientist. I drew up plans for my home, Monticello, and helped design our nation's Capitol. I set up schools for my state, and I founded the University of Virginia.

I had great wealth, so I decided to quit my law practice and devote myself to serving my country. I became a leader of the American Revolution, and I wrote the Declaration of Independence.

I became secretary of state, Vice President, and later the third President of the United States. During my presidency, the Louisiana Purchase was made and the Lewis and Clark expedition was launched.

I worked for liberty and the rights of the people.

Who was I?

JOHN PAUL JONES (1747-1792)

I was born in Scotland in 1747. At the age of twelve I became a sailor and sailed to America. Between voyages I stayed in Virginia with my brother. It was there that I heard the Americans talk of freedom. I knew that I wanted to join the colonists in their fight.

I became a captain in America's new navy. I was able to acquire an old ship which I named the *Bonhomme Richard* (Good Man Richard), in honor of Benjamin Franklin, who wrote *Poor Richard's Almanac.*

During a famous battle with the English ship *Serapis*, the British commander asked me if I was ready to surrender. I replied, "I have not yet begun to fight!" The battle continued. Both ships were on fire. Finally the British ship surrendered.

During the Revolutionary War I captured over 300 English ships. I was America's first naval hero.

Who was I?

ROBERT E. LEE (1807-1870)

I was born in Virginia in 1807. My parents were a fine, well-known family. I had everything that a good home could offer. I attended the U.S. Military Academy at West Point, where I became interested in engineering.

When my state of Virginia left the Union, it took me many hours to decide what to do. I finally decided to leave the U.S. Army and to fight for my state.

During the Civil War I led the Southern forces. On April 8, 1865, when it was evident that the South had lost the war, I surrendered to General Grant at Appomattox. After the war I did my best to establish friendship between the North and the South.

I was an engineer, a soldier, and the leader of the Southern armies during the Civil War.

Who was I?

ABRAHAM LINCOLN (1809-1865)

I was born in a log cabin in Kentucky in 1809. When I was nine my mother died.

I wasn't able to attend school regularly. In all, I attended about a year. I did learn to read and write, and after that I taught myself. Later I was elected to the Illinois Legislature. After becoming a lawyer, I was elected to Congress.

When running for the Senate, Stephen Douglas and I had a debate about slavery that made us both famous. Douglas wanted slavery to remain. I thought that whether the country should be slave or free was not the most important thing to consider. Keeping our country undivided was the main concern. I said, "A house divided against itself cannot stand."

As a result of the debates with Stephen Douglas, in 1861 I became President of the United States. The Civil War began one month after I became President. In order to shorten the war and save many lives, I freed the slaves in 1863.

During the dedication of a national cemetery at Gettysburg I gave a short speech, which has since been considered one of the greatest speeches ever made in American history. It is known as the Gettysburg Address.

The Civil War ended one month after I began my second term as president. I was looking forward to bringing all the states together and strengthening the Union, but one night in a theater in Washington, D.C., I was shot by a half-crazed actor. I died the next day.

I am considered one of America's greatest Presidents.

Who was I?

TOM PAINE (1737-1809)

I was born in 1737 in Norfolk, England. In 1774 I came to America, sponsored by my idol, Benjamin Franklin.

In my pamphlet *Common Sense,* I argued for American independence. When the Revolutionary War began, I wrote *The American Crisis.* In that work I said, "These are the times that try men's souls. The summer soldier and the sunshine patriot will, in this crisis, shrink from the service of their country." George Washington ordered that the pamphlet be read to his soldiers.

My writings greatly influenced the leaders of the American Revolution. I also became famous in France during the French Revolution. I have been described as an "Englishman by birth, French citizen by decree, and American by adoption."

I was an American Revolutionary writer and pamphleteer.

Who was I?

POCAHONTAS (1595?-1617)

I was the daughter of Powhatan, an American Indian chief. When I was twelve my father was about to kill Captain John Smith with a club. I placed my head upon Captain Smith's and begged my father not to kill him.

When fighting between the white settlers and the Indians broke out, I was captured. I fell in love with a white settler, married him, was converted to Christianity, and was baptized with the English name Rebecca. When I moved to London the English thought that I was an Indian princess. I died of smallpox while waiting to sail back to America.

I am best remembered for saving the life of Captain John Smith.

Who was I?

PAUL REVERE (1735-1818)

I was born in Massachusetts in 1735. I was trained in the silversmith's trade at an early age. My work brought me into contact with such patriots as John Hancock and Samuel Adams. I participated in the Boston Tea Party in 1773. I often rode horseback to carry news to waiting patriots. My most famous ride was the time I arranged for a signal of lights to be placed in the North Church steeple to warn of the British approach. The signal was "one if by land and two if by sea." Henry Wadsworth Longfellow wrote a poem about my ride.

I was an American craftsman and patriot.

Who was I?

THEODORE ROOSEVELT (1858-1919)

I was born in New York City in 1858 to a family of wealth. I was a sickly child and was taught at home because I was not well enough to go to school. I worked in a gymnasium to build up my body. By the time I was ready to attend college, my health had improved enough that I was able to go.

Later I was elected to the New York State Legislature. In 1897 I became assistant secretary of the Navy. During the Spanish-American War, I left my job and gathered a group of soldiers to fight in Cuba. The soldiers were called Rough Riders. After leading my Rough Riders into battle up San Juan Hill, I became a national hero.

I served as governor of New York, Vice President of the United States, and President of the United States. As President I worked for conservation of our trees. I had the Panama Canal built. I broke up monopolies and sponsored laws for healthy food and workers' compensation. I helped establish our national parks. I believed in a strong military.

One of my famous remarks was, "Speak softly and carry a big stick."

I was a man of adventure. I traveled in Africa, Europe, and South America. I was a rancher, a soldier, a big game hunter, and one of America's best-loved presidents.

Who was I?

BETSY ROSS (1752-1836)

I was born in Philadelphia in 1752, the daughter of a Quaker carpenter. When I grew up I married an upholsterer. Shortly thereafter my husband was killed. I took his shop over and became an expert seamstress.

In June 1776 a committee headed by George Washington visited me. The committee asked me to make a new flag for America, which I did. It was the first American flag that had stars and stripes.

I was a seamstress who made flags during the American Revolution.
Who was I?

SACAJAWEA (1787?-1812?)

I was born among the Shoshone Indians of Idaho about 1787. After I was captured by enemy Indians, I was sold as a slave. My owner and I joined the Lewis and Clark Expedition, and I became the expedition's main guide. Together we explored the wilderness from Illinois to the Pacific Coast of Oregon.

I have been honored by having a river, a peak, and a mountain pass named after me. My name means Bird Woman.
Who was I?

UNCLE SAM

I am a symbol of the people and government of the United States of America. As a visual representation of the government, I often appear in parades and am pictured in books, magazines, and newspapers. I am usually seen wearing a white beard and a tall hat in red, white, and blue.

I represent the qualities of the American people. I am honest, hard-working, and good-hearted. I also represent the federal government. I look after the people wisely and with good will.

I represent the affection and loyalty you have for our people and government.
Who am I?

BOOKER T. WASHINGTON (1856-1915)

I was born a slave in Virginia in 1856. After the slaves were freed, my family moved to West Virginia. I was largely self-educated, but I rose to found a school for Negroes named Tuskegee Institute, where I served as principal until I died.

I urged African Americans to stop demanding equal rights. I felt that if they worked hard and acquired property, their rights would eventually be granted. I advised them to obey the laws and to make friends with whites.

I started an organization to help Negroes develop their own businesses. I raised money for Negro schools. Among the several books I wrote, my autobiography, *Up from Slavery,* was the most famous.

I was a Negro educator, and, in my time, I became the best-known Negro in the United States.

Who was I?

GEORGE WASHINGTON (1732-1799)

I was born in Virginia on February 22, 1732. During my youth I lived on a plantation and spent much time outside. Later I became a surveyor.

During the French and Indian War I was an Army commander. Several times I nearly lost my life. In one battle my coat showed four bullet holes. Two horses were shot from under me. Several years later, because of poor health, I retired to my home, Mount Vernon.

Sometime thereafter I returned to the Army as commander-in-chief and led the colonists against the British in the Revolutionary War. One winter my troops and I camped at Valley Forge, where we experienced terrible hardships. We did not have enough food or proper clothing. Many soldiers' feet froze and bled. Sickness spread, and many men died.

After we won the Revolutionary War, I was elected first President of the United States. The capital of our country, Washington, D.C., is named for me.

It is said that I was first in war, first in peace, and first in the hearts of my countrymen.

Who was I?

DANIEL WEBSTER (1782-1852)

I was born in New Hampshire in 1782. When I was a boy I enjoyed camping, hunting, and fishing. I loved to read, and I could often recite long passages that I had read.

I became a lawyer and was chosen to represent Massachusetts in Congress. A speech I made before Congress will always be remembered. It ends with these words: "Liberty and Union, now and forever, one and inseparable!"

I tried to help solve the problem of slavery that was facing our country. I hated slavery, but I wanted to preserve the Union at all costs. During the great debate of 1850 I spoke in favor of a compromise to the country's problems. I helped prevent war between the North and South for a time.

I was famous for my speeches. I was a leader and a patriot.

Who was I?

II
Famous American Writers

Illustrated by
Geraldine Hulbert

Use of the Puppets

Teacher/Librarian Use

Some ways of using the Famous American Writers puppets are as follows:
1. To introduce or enrich a unit, book, research, or biography. For example,
   - Read a chapter a day from Laura Ingalls Wilder's *The Little House on the Prairie* or present the work on video. Some time thereafter, present the author's puppet and the biographical riddle as a review or enrichment.
   - Assign students to make, research, and present puppets of the famous American writers in this chapter. If there are more students in the class than there are authors, besides listing the authors, also list one or more of the authors' literary works. Some students should present puppets and biographical reports. Each of the other students should present a puppet and a review of an author's book. (This results in an author's puppet being presented more than once.) An alternative would be to introduce two chapters of puppets and combine their biographies onto one list for presentation.
2. To review famous American writers covered in the social studies or English curriculum
3. To culminate a unit in which famous American writers figure prominently
4. To enrich a bulletin board display of student reports or book jackets about famous American writers

Student Use

Students may research, make, and present the puppets.

Recreational Use

The puppets may be used in recreational settings, such as at camp, at home, etc.

Louisa May Alcott

Stephen Crane

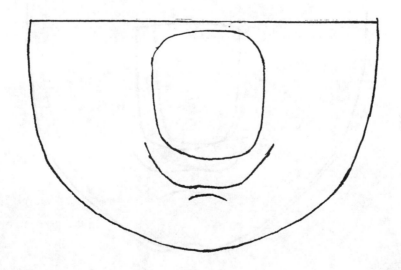

Emily Dickinson

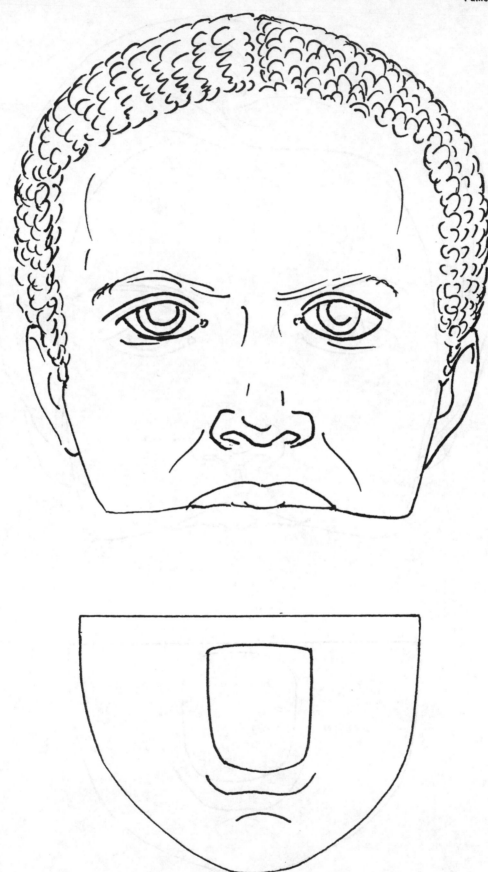

Paul Laurence Dunbar

Ralph Waldo Emerson

Jean Craighead George

Nathaniel Hawthorne

Washington Irving

Henry Wadsworth Longfellow

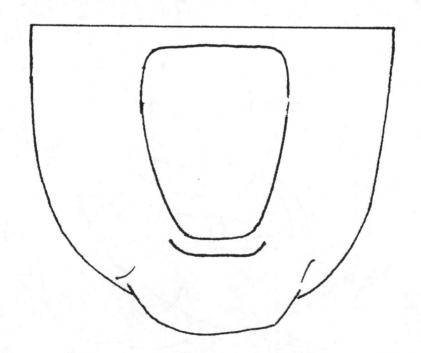

Edgar Allan Poe

Henry David Thoreau

Mark Twain

Walt Whitman

John Greenleaf Whittier

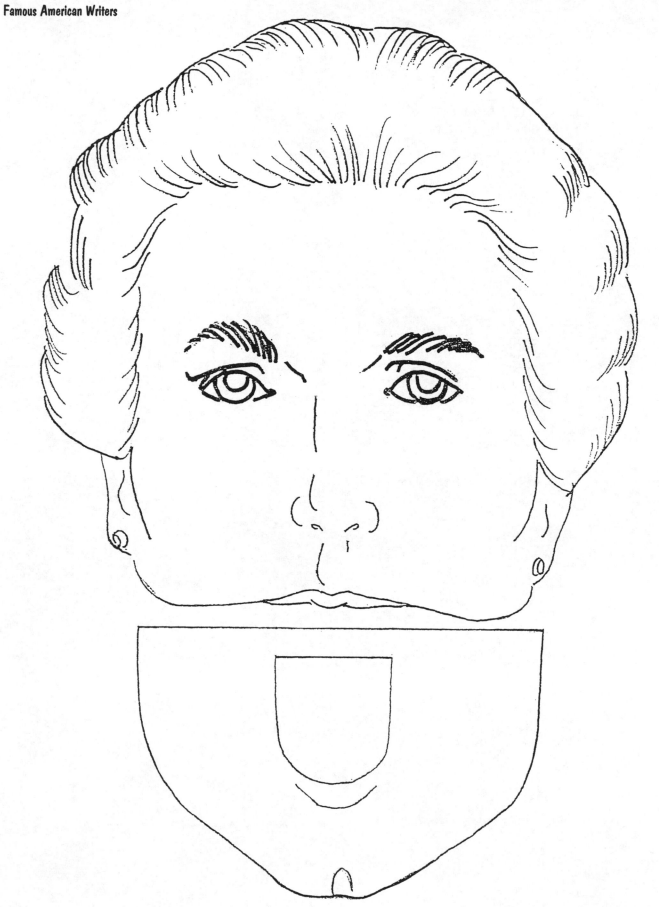

Laura Ingalls Wilder

Riddles to Use with the Puppets

These riddles, which provide basic biographical information, may be told by either the instructor or by the students. If students are presenting the puppets, the instructor may let the students use the riddles in this book or may choose to have students do research and make up their own riddles. In a presentation, the puppet's name is withheld. The manipulator tells a riddle and at the conclusion chooses a student to identify the puppet.

LOUISA MAY ALCOTT (1832-1888)

I was born in Pennsylvania in 1832. Most of my life was spent around Boston and Concord, Massachusetts. My father was a philosopher, writer, and teacher.

At sixteen I started a little school. It was not successful, but a book I wrote for my students turned out to be the first of my books to be published. A publishing house asked me to write a story for girls. I hesitated, but agreed to try. I wrote *Little Women,* a book about my own family. Its publication provided my family with both comfort and security. I later wrote *Little Men, Jo's Boys,* and several other books.

I am remembered especially for writing *Little Women,* one of the best-loved stories in American literature.

Who was I?

STEPHEN CRANE (1871-1900)

I was born in 1871, the youngest of a Methodist minister's fourteen children. As a youngster I was interested in baseball, the theater, and the reading and writing of novels.

For five years I worked as a freelance writer. My first book, a failure, was published in 1893 at my own expense. Shortly thereafter my book about the Civil War, *The Red Badge of Courage,* brought spectacular fame.

Because of poor health and also because of gossip about my private life, I moved to England. Shortly I found myself deeply in debt. Although I tried to write myself out of debt, I was unsuccessful. Plagued by tuberculosis, I died in Germany at the age of twenty-nine.

Who was I?

EMILY DICKINSON (1830-1886)

I was born in Massachusetts in 1830. In my youth, I was a happy, sociable, and rather rebellious young lady.

When my father was elected to the House of Representatives, he sent for my mother, my sisters, and me to share the social life of Washington. On our way home we stopped in Philadelphia and heard the famous Dr. Wadsworth preach. He became very important to me, but he was not free to marry. Since

I could not marry the man of my choice, I never married. I withdrew more and more from society.

Only one of my poems was published during my life. The others were found in a dresser drawer.

I am one of America's greatest poets.

Who was I?

PAUL LAURENCE DUNBAR (1872-1906)

I was born in 1872. My mother, who had been a slave in her youth, remembered the stories and poems her master had read aloud, and she told them to me. My father had also been a slave. He was a difficult man, who left the family and never returned. Because of poor health, I was allowed to stay in school while my brothers went to work. My first book of poetry, which I dedicated to my mother, was published in 1892. In repayment for all my mother's sacrifices, I bought her a little house.

Although I had many low points in my life, I also had many high points. During my life I published four novels, many stories, and some books of poems. I gradually achieved recognition and came to be known as "the poet laureate of the Negro race."

Who was I?

RALPH WALDO EMERSON (1803-1882)

I was born in Boston in 1803, a descendant of eight generations of ministers.

When my father died, my mother found it difficult to provide for her five sons. Although plagued by poor health and poverty, I entered Harvard College. By age twenty-three I was prepared to preach. Although I was successful as a minister, my views changed, and I resigned from the ministry.

When I was thirty-eight my first volume of essays was published. Lecturing and writing, I had little time for social activities. However, I was interested in important issues of the day. I spoke on behalf of the antislavery movement and I supported women's suffrage.

Typical of my thought was this statement: "Though we travel the world over to find the beautiful, we must carry it with us or we find it not." I became famous all over the world and was considered one of the most original thinkers of the nineteenth century.

Who was I?

JEAN CRAIGHEAD GEORGE (1919-   )

I was born in 1919 in Washington, D.C. I grew up loving nature and would spend hours sitting on the forest floor studying insects, plants, and animals. During my life I've kept 173 wild animals as pets, all of which I allowed to leave when they were ready to go. Many of the animals became characters in my books and other writings.

I am the author of over sixty books, some of which I illustrated myself. Most of my books are about animals or about young people who have learned to survive in the wilderness. *Julie of the Wolves* is about a lost Eskimo girl who survived by learning to live with wolves. The book won the 1973 Newbery Medal. *My Side of the Mountain,* the story of a boy who runs away to the woods to live a year, was a 1960 Newbery Honor book.

I have won numerous awards for my books about nature, about survival in the wilderness. and about children searching for independence and self-knowledge.

Who am I?

NATHANIEL HAWTHORNE (1804-1864)

I was born in Salem, Massachusetts, in 1804, the only son of a sea captain. My mother, crushed by my father's death when I was four, shut herself away from society for the rest of her life—forty years.

When I was thirty-eight, I married Sophia Peabody, with whom I had long been in love. Although we had very little money, we were extremely happy.

I considered myself the most unpopular writer in America because I had been able to sell very few of my writings. When I was forty-six my fortune changed. *The Scarlet Letter* became an immediate success and brought wide recognition. *The House of the Seven Gables,* shortly thereafter, also became a favorite.

I traveled abroad with my family, wrote, and enjoyed life. I was considered America's first great novelist.

Who was I?

WASHINGTON IRVING (1783-1859)

I was born in 1783 in New York City. I loved to read, but my greatest longing was to see the world.

When I was twenty-five, the woman to whom I was engaged to marry died. I never fully got over her death, and I remained a bachelor all my life.

At age thirty-six I decided to try to earn a living by writing. In 1819 and 1820 I wrote *The Sketch Book,* which was very successful. It included my two most important works: "Rip Van Winkle" and "The Legend of Sleepy Hollow."

I began writing five volumes of *The Life of Washington* when I was sixty-seven and finished a very short time before I died, nine years later. I overcame much in my life: poverty, ill-health, and sorrow, but I lived to taste victory.

I was acclaimed as America's first man of letters.

Who was I?

HENRY WADSWORTH LONGFELLOW (1807-1882)

I was born in Maine in 1807. At nineteen I graduated from college and afterwards traveled in Europe for three years. When I came home to teach, I fell in love and married. While my wife and I were abroad, she took ill and died.

I became a professor and wrote in my free time. By the time I was forty-seven, my books were selling so well that I quit teaching and gave my time to writing.

I married again and had six children. I wrote a number of poems about children and became known as "The Children's Poet." Among the writings for which I am famous are *Evangeline*, *Hiawatha*, and *The Courtship of Miles Standish*.

Although my life was touched by tragedy, on the whole, I lived a happy seventy-five years. Unlike most poets, who were often poor and struggling, I always knew comfort and ease.

I was America's best-known poet, more famous in my lifetime than any other poet.

Who was I?

EDGAR ALLAN POE (1809-1849)

I was born in Boston in 1809 to parents who were always on the verge of poverty. I was orphaned at three.

When I grew up, I decided to devote my life to writing. My wife suffered ill-health and due to anxiety about her and also due to the effects of my drinking, I often changed jobs. When my wife died, I was broken. I used liquor as a means to escape my despair, but it only increased my problems.

As an author, I was recognized for my skill as a short story writer and for inventing the modern detective story. I am also known for my tales of mystery, horror, the supernatural, and the fantastic. I am especially remembered for my poems "The Raven," "The Bells," and "Annabel Lee" and for such stories as "The Gold Bug," "The Purloined Letter," and "The Pit and the Pendulum."

Ill, depressed, and drinking, I died penniless in 1849. I have been called the saddest figure in American literature.

Who was I?

HENRY DAVID THOREAU (1817-1862)

I was born in Concord, Massachusetts, in 1817. After graduating from Harvard in 1837, I worked as a teacher, surveyor, engineer, carpenter, and gardener.

I was completely at home in the open. I spent two years in a hut that I built in the Walden woods. My best-known book, *Walden*, is a record of those years. During my lifetime of forty-five years, only two of my books were published. They were *A Week on the Concord and Merrimac Rivers* and *Walden*.

I was a writer, naturalist, and philosopher. *Walden*, my best-loved book, is one of the most widely read American classics.

Who was I?

MARK TWAIN (1835-1910)

I was born in Missouri in 1835. I became a printer, a river pilot, and a writer. Some of my writing was so popular that I decided to see if I could succeed as a lecturer. My attempt at lecturing was a huge success. I married and had three daughters. I had a number of unfortunate business ventures. Tragedy also struck me when my wife and two of my daughters died.

I wrote two of America's most famous books: *The Adventures of Tom Sawyer* and *Huckleberry Finn.* My real name was Samuel Langhorne Clemens, but you probably know me by my pen name.

Great public honors were bestowed on me, but I was also well acquainted with sorrow. I am considered the greatest humorist in American literature.

Who was I?

WALT WHITMAN (1819-1892)

I was born in New York in 1819, the second of nine children.

In 1842 I entered my career of creative writing. I also worked as a printer, store manager, and building contractor. I couldn't find a commercial publisher who would accept my book *Leaves of Grass,* so I printed it at my own expense. I was stricken with paralysis. Shortly thereafter my beloved mother died. I never fully recovered from either of these tragedies.

When the sale of my poems boomed, I was able to buy a small house where I lived until my death in 1892.

My poems were in praise of the United States and of democracy, but as I wrote in the preface of one of my books "the United States themselves are essentially the greatest poem." My book of poems entitled *Leaves of Grass* is considered one of the world's major literary works.

Who was I?

JOHN GREENLEAF WHITTIER (1807-1892)

I was born on a farm in Massachusetts in 1807. When my schooling was over, I wrote and edited for awhile.

I fought slavery for thirty years, even though my life was often endangered. My health was poor, but even so I turned out a book of poems almost every year. Two of my most famous poems were "Snowbound" and "The Barefoot Boy."

I was always interested in politics and religion. Twice I was elected to the State Legislature. Although my life began in poverty and obscurity, it ended in comfort and fame.

I was the most loved poet of America.

Who was I?

LAURA INGALLS WILDER (1867-1957)

I was born in Wisconsin in 1867. From our Little House in the Big Woods, my parents, sisters, and I traveled into Indian Territory, where we lived in the Little House on the Prairie. Years later, in Dakota Territory, I trained as a school teacher and then married.

When I was sixty years old, my daughter suggested that I write down memories of my childhood and of growing up. Based upon my recollections of the pioneering family life I lived during the 1870s and 1880s, I wrote nine novels for children. Among the series were *Little House in the Big Woods, Little House on the Prairie, On the Banks of Plum Creek, By the Shores of Silver Lake, The Long Winter,* and *Little Town on the Prairie. The Little House on the Prairie* TV series, which began in 1974 and is still telecast in reruns, was based on parts of my books.

Who was I?

III

Famous Women

Illustrated by
Cynthia Johnson

Use of the Puppets

Teacher/Librarian Use

Some ways of using Famous Women puppets are as follows:
1. To introduce a unit, story, research, or biography
2. To review famous women covered in the social studies or English curriculum
3. To culminate a unit in which famous women figure prominently
4. To feature a famous woman in relation to a specific event
   - Election Day—After discussing that there will be an election in the city/state/nation, explain briefly what the term "election" means and who/what will be voted on. Then you might say something like this: "Let's go back into history and meet someone who was very important in bringing about one of our voting laws." (Present the Susan B. Anthony puppet and the biographical material in the riddle about her. If students are likely to identify the puppet, end with "Who was I?" If not, end with "My name was Susan B. Anthony.")
   - Black History Month—After discussing the meaning of Black History Month, you might say something like this: "Let's go back many years ago and meet a woman who was important in black history." (Present the Harriet Tubman puppet and the biographical material in the riddle about her. If students are likely to identify the puppet, end with "Who was I?" If not, end by saying, "My name was Harriet Tubman.")
5. To enrich a bulletin board display of student reports or a display of book jackets about famous women

Student Use

Students may research, make, and present the puppets.

Recreational Use

The puppets may be used in recreational settings, such as at camp, at home, etc.

Susan B. Anthony

Elizabeth Blackwell

Nellie Bly

Cleopatra

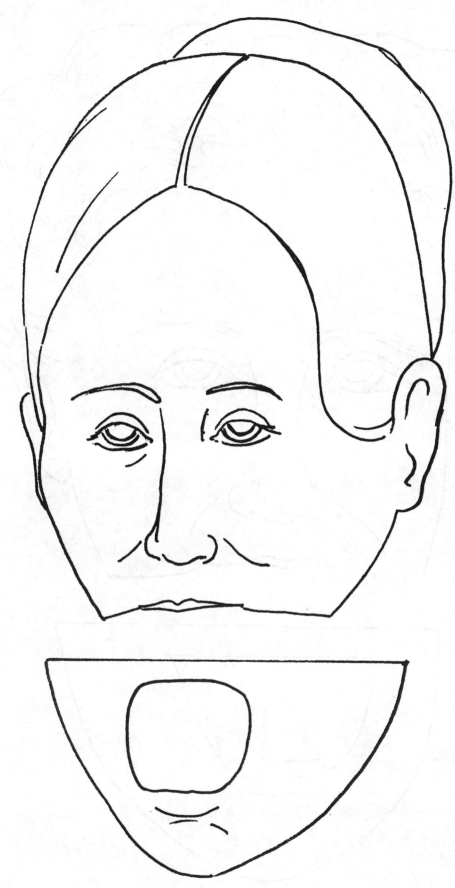

Dorothea Lynde Dix

Mary Baker Eddy

Joan of Arc

Florence Nightingale

Molly Pitcher

Harriet Tubman

Narcissa Whitman

Riddles to Use with the Puppets

These riddles, which provide basic biographical information, may be told by either the instructor or by the students. If students are presenting the puppets, the instructor may let the students use the riddles in this book or may choose to have students do research and make up their own riddles. In a presentation, the puppet's name is withheld. The manipulator tells a riddle and at the conclusion chooses a student to identify the puppet.

SUSAN B. ANTHONY (1820-1906)

I was born in Massachusetts in 1820, the daughter of Quaker parents. My father appreciated my abilities and sent me to a school where I could learn more than girls were usually taught. In 1837 when my father lost his cotton mill, I was forced to get a job. I got a position as a teacher at a salary of $2.50 a week.

After becoming convinced that women should be allowed to vote, I decided to devote my life to that cause. One election day I did a startling thing: I went to a polling place and before I could be stopped, I cast a vote. For this I was arrested and fined $100. However, news of the case swept through the country, and I became an honored spokesperson for the rights of women.

More than any other person, I laid the groundwork for giving women the right to vote. However, it was fourteen years after my death before that right was established.

Who was I?

ELIZABETH BLACKWELL (1821-1910)

I was born in England in 1821. In 1832 I moved to New York City.

Later I taught school for five years and then decided to become a doctor. After graduating from medical school, I became the first woman doctor in the United States. When I began my practice, I was an outcast in the medical profession. However, the poor flocked to me when I opened a small hospital in the slums.

Although I agreed with most medical practices, I opposed vaccination and operating on living animals for research.

I helped break down prejudice against women in medicine and in other professions.

Who was I?

NELLIE BLY (1867?-1922)

I was born in Pennsylvania about 1867. At the age of eighteen I wrote a letter to a newspaper supporting women's rights. The editor of the paper liked my writing so much that he hired me as a reporter.

Wanting to learn how the police treated women prisoners, I pretended to be a thief and got arrested. Another time I pretended to be insane so I could get inside a mental hospital. Reforms often followed the exposés I wrote.

In 1889 my newspaper assigned me to try to outdo the hero of Jules Verne's book, *Around the World in Eighty Days.* Traveling by ship, train, hand cart, and burro, I made the trip in 72 days, 6 hours, and 11 minutes.

I adopted my pen name, by which you know me, from a song by Stephen Foster. My real name was Elizabeth Cochrane Seaman. I was an American journalist known for the daring exposés I wrote.

Who was I?

CLEOPATRA (69 B.C.-30 B.C.)

The most famous of all the Egyptian queens, I was born over 2,000 years ago in 69 B.C. At seventeen, when I became queen and co-ruler with my brother, I was forced into exile.

When Julius Caesar came to Egypt, I decided to ask him to help me get my share of power back. Fearful of my brother's soldiers, I wrapped myself in a rug and was carried into the palace on the shoulders of a servant. Caesar promised to help me. My brother drowned, and a younger brother and I took the throne.

When Caesar invited me to visit Rome, I went and stayed until Caesar was assassinated.

I married a friend of Caesar's: Mark Anthony. After Anthony was defeated in a war with Octavius, he committed suicide. I tried unsuccessfully to bring Octavius under a spell. Fearing that Octavius would put me to death, I had a servant bring a deadly snake to me. Submitting to the bite of the snake, I died at the age of thirty-eight.

Who was I?

DOROTHEA LYNDE DIX (1802-1887)

I was born in Maine in 1802. In my twenties I became a teacher. I joined the Unitarian Church, studied the Bible, and tried to develop myself morally and spiritually.

I volunteered to teach a Sunday School class at a jail. There among the criminals and drunkards I found some mentally ill people who were being mistreated. Through my efforts, most abuses to the mentally ill were corrected in my state.

I inspected 300 jails, 500 poorhouses, and numerous prisons. Everywhere I went I continued to find mentally ill people who were being mistreated. I traveled 60,000 miles awakening people to this problem. One hundred twenty-three asylums and hospitals were built through my efforts. For the last fifty years of my life I had no home. I often lived in the hospitals I had established.

I labored most of my life to help the mentally ill.

Who was I?

MARY BAKER EDDY (1821-1910)

I was born in New Hampshire in 1821, the youngest of six children. My parents were religious people who made the Bible a very important part of life.

In 1866 I fell on an icy pavement, became unconscious, and was not expected to live. Three days later I opened my Bible and from the spiritual understanding gained from my reading, I was healed.

Thereafter I dedicated my life to the spiritual method of healing which I had discovered. I named this method Christian Science. Its basis is "there is no matter, all is Mind." I wrote, among other books, a textbook which set forth the principles of spiritual healing. I founded the Christian Science Church, a publishing house, and several periodicals.

I was the only woman to found a major religion. In October 1995 I was inducted into the National Women's Hall of Fame.

Who was I?

JOAN OF ARC (1412-1431)

I was born in France in 1412, the daughter of a farmer. Visions and voices frequently came to me. The voices told me to put on armor and become a captain in the wars, for I was chosen by God to save France.

After much pleading to see the Dauphin, the oldest son of the king, he summoned me. Being suspicious, he had an impostor sit on the throne and he stood in humble clothes with the servants. Although I had never seen him before, I went right to him and fell on my knees. After I was given a sword and armor, I led the attacks on the English. Orleans was saved and the Dauphin was crowned king.

Later in battle, I was taken prisoner. The English bought me, and in 1431 they burned me at the stake. Twenty-five years later I was pronounced innocent of the charges of the English, and nearly 500 years later I was made a saint.

Who was I?

FLORENCE NIGHTINGALE (1820-1910)

I was born in 1820 in Italy, in the city of Florence, after which I was named. My family moved to England shortly after my birth.

When I grew up I became a nurse, which was unusual for a woman of refinement. The government asked me to go to the Crimea where war was raging and reorganize hospitals there. I took thirty women with me. This was the first time women were to care for soldiers fallen in war. Before we arrived, the death rate was 60%, after we arrived it was 1%.

After the war I remained until the last soldier was sent home, and then I followed him. I lived for many years thereafter. I founded a home for the training of nurses and was indirectly responsible for the birth of the Red Cross.

Who was I?

MOLLY PITCHER (1754?-1832)

I was born in Philadelphia about 1754. During the American Revolutionary War, I wondered why men got a chance to fight for their country, but women didn't. I wished that I were a man so I could wear a uniform and bear arms myself.

After I married, I followed my husband to the battlefield. When I saw soldiers overcome by heat and thirst, I grabbed a bucket and ran and filled it in a stream. As soon as I gave water to one soldier, another would say, "Molly, the pitcher! Please!"

All day during battle I carried water to the hot, the thirsty, and the wounded. When my husband fell forward on his cannon, the general ordered the cannon removed because there was no one to take my husband's place. I ran to the gun, loaded it, and fired. For hours I toiled with the cannon. Finally our forces claimed victory. The general shook my hand and thanked me in the name of the American Army. I had fulfilled my dream: I had become a soldier.

Who was I?

HARRIET TUBMAN (1820?-1913)

I was born in slavery in Maryland about 1820. At the age of five I was a housekeeping helper and a baby sitter. Later I worked on the grounds and in the fields. Learning that I was to be sent away to a chain gang, I escaped to the North where I could be free. Thereafter for twenty years I helped slaves escape by way of the Underground Railroad, a network of escape routes.

I could not read or write, but I could talk, and I was greatly sought as a speaker by those opposed to slavery.

During the Civil War I was a spy, a nurse, and a scout for the Northern forces. I personally made nineteen trips to the South and led three hundred fugitives out. I was known as "the Moses of my people."

Who was I?

NARCISSA WHITMAN (1808-1847)

I was born in New York in 1808. From the age of twelve I dreamed of being a missionary to the Indians. During my life I was able to fulfill that dream.

When I married, my husband and I decided to set out across the Rocky Mountains and go into Oregon to establish a mission. My husband, a doctor, wanted to teach the Indians how to stay healthy. I wanted to teach them about God.

It was a long, hard, dangerous trip to Oregon. We walked across plains, forded rivers, and fought off stampeding buffalo. After arriving at our destination we built a Mission House in which we conducted religious, educational, and medical activities. During the year of 1846, sixty-nine men, women, and children crowded into our mission needing care. Each year the number grew.

In 1847 my husband and I, and several of our adopted children, were killed by non-Christian Cayuse Indians. The last words that I ever spoke were, "Tell my sister that I died at my post."

Who was I?

IV
Famous Presidents

Illustrated by
Harvey H. Lively

Use of the Puppets

Teacher/Librarian Use

Some ways of using the Famous Presidents puppets are as follows:

1. To introduce a unit, story, research, or biography
2. To review famous presidents covered in the social studies curriculum
3. To culminate a unit in which famous presidents figure prominently
4. To feature a famous president in relation to a specific event
   - Abraham Lincoln's Birthday—Present the Abraham Lincoln puppet and riddle. If desired, have each student make an Abraham Lincoln puppet
   - George Washington's Birthday—Present the George Washington puppet and riddle. If desired, have each student make a George Washington puppet
5. To enrich a bulletin board display of student reports or a display of book jackets about famous presidents

Student Use

Students may research, make, and present the puppets.

Recreational Use

The puppets may be used in recreational settings, such as at camp, at home, etc.

Note

See the index under Presidents for the location of additional puppets.

John Adams

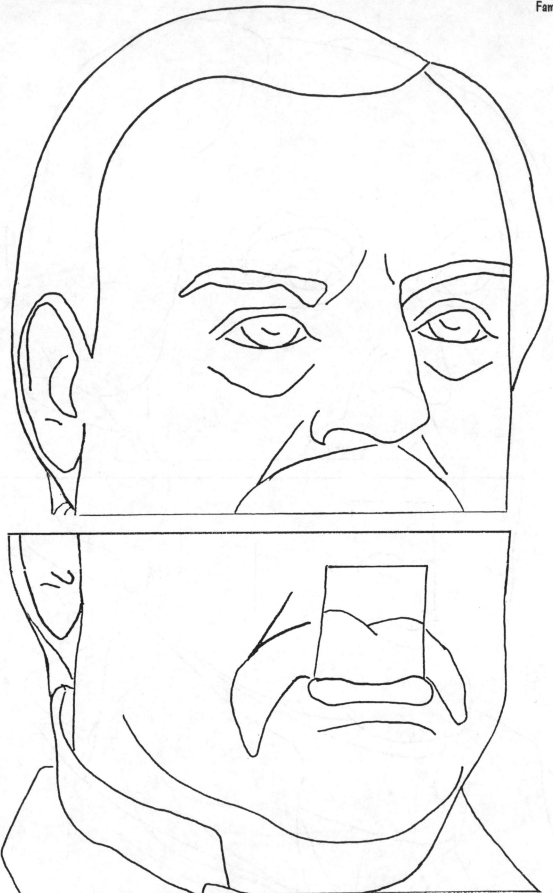

Grover Cleveland

Andrew Jackson

Thomas Jefferson

Abraham Lincoln

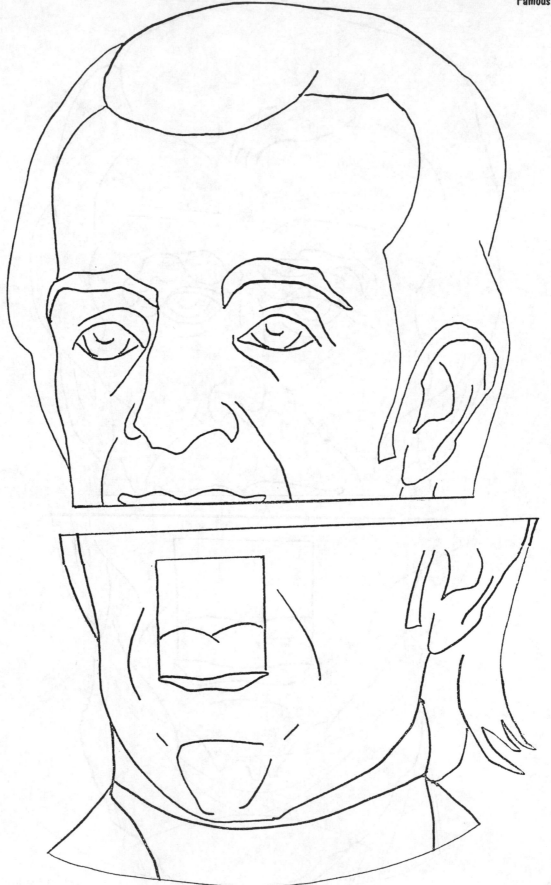

James Polk

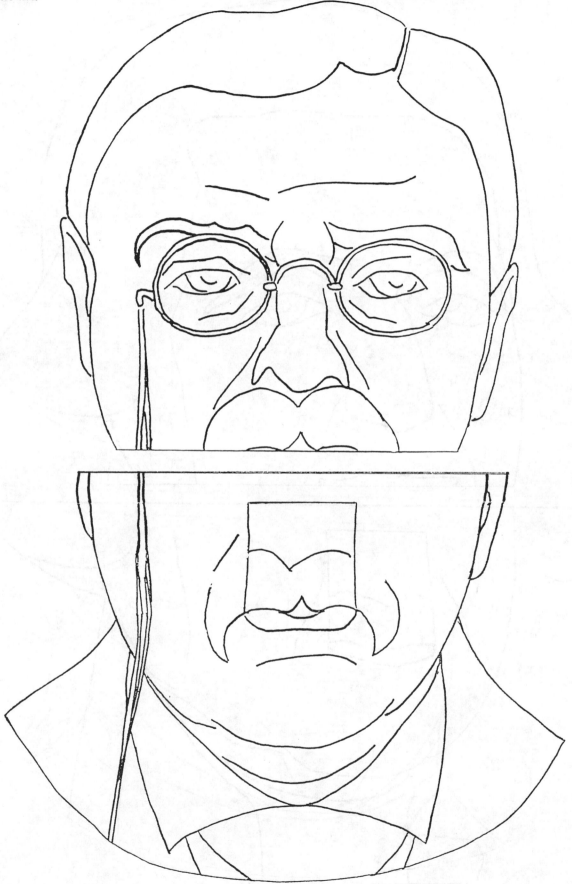

Theodore Roosevelt

George Washington

Riddles to Use with the Puppets

These riddles, which provide basic biographical information, may be told by either the instructor or by the students. If students are presenting the puppets, the instructor may let the students use the riddles in this book or may choose to have students do research and make up their own riddles. In a presentation, the puppet's name is withheld. The manipulator tells a riddle and at the conclusion chooses a student to identify the puppet.

JOHN ADAMS (1735-1826)

I was born in Massachusetts in 1735. As a youth I was trained to uphold high standards. I was honest, thrifty, religious, and obedient to my parents. I took the responsibility that went with wealth and education seriously.

Before I was twenty I graduated from college. I became a teacher, a lawyer, and a member of the Continental Congress. Later I became the first Vice President of the United States. In 1796 I became the second President of the United States. Avoiding war with France was one of my major accomplishments.

I lived to see my son become the sixth President of the United States. When asked to give a toast for a Fourth of July celebration, I replied: "Independence Forever!"

Who was I?

GROVER CLEVELAND (1837-1908)

I was born in New Jersey in 1837, the son of a minister. During my life I was a lawyer, sheriff, mayor, governor, and the twenty-second and the twenty-fourth President of the United States.

A bachelor when I became President, I was the first and only president to marry in the White House. As President, I stood for a lower tariff and for money based on the gold standard. I strengthened the Civil Service Act of 1883 and signed into law the Interstate Commerce Act.

When I returned to the White House as twenty-fourth President, I inherited a sick country. The Panic of 1893, marked by hundreds of bank failures, thousands of bankruptcies, and mass unemployment, troubled my second administration. Before dying in 1908, my last recorded words were: "I have tried so hard to do the right."

At the age of forty-four I was almost unknown. At forty-eight I was President of the United States.

Who was I?

ANDREW JACKSON (1767-1845)

In 1767 I was born near the border between North and South Carolina. My father and mother died while I was young. Thereafter, I found work to support myself, and later I studied law and became a lawyer.

I moved to Tennessee, served actively in state and federal government, and became one of Tennessee's most important citizens. I won fame as an Indian fighter, and I served at the Battle of New Orleans.

In 1828 I was elected President of the United States. Because I was as strong in mind and body as hickory wood, I was called "Old Hickory." I spent my last years at my beautful home, The Hermitage.

Who was I?

THOMAS JEFFERSON (1743-1826)

I was born in Virginia in 1743. My father, a pioneer, taught me never to ask another to do for me what I could do for myself. I learned to ride a horse, shoot a gun, paddle a canoe, and hunt.

I began studying when I was five years old, and I studied all my life. I played the violin. I was a farmer, surveyor, lawyer, and scientist. I drew up plans for my home, Monticello, and helped design our nation's Capitol. I set up schools for my state, and I founded the University of Virginia.

I had great wealth, so I decided to quit my law practice and devote myself to serving my country. I became a leader of the American Revolution, and I wrote the Declaration of Independence.

I became secretary of state, Vice President, and later the third President of the United States. During my presidency, the Louisiana Purchase was made and the Lewis and Clark expedition was launched.

I worked for liberty and the rights of the people.

Who was I?

ABRAHAM LINCOLN (1809-1865)

I was born in a log cabin in Kentucky in 1809. When I was nine my mother died.

I wasn't able to attend school regularly. In all, I attended about a year. I did learn to read and write, and after that I taught myself. Later I was elected to the Illinois Legislature. After becoming a lawyer, I was elected to Congress.

When running for the Senate, Stephen Douglas and I had a debate about slavery that made us both famous. Douglas wanted slavery to remain. I thought that whether the country should be slave or free was not the most important thing to consider. Keeping our country undivided was the main concern. I said, "A house divided against itself cannot stand."

As a result of the debates with Stephen Douglas, in 1861 I became President of the United States. The Civil War began one month after I became President. In order to shorten the war and save many lives, I freed the slaves in 1863.

During the dedication of a national cemetery at Gettysburg I gave a short speech, which has since been considered one of the greatest speeches ever made in American history. It is known as the Gettysburg Address.

The Civil War ended one month after I began my second term as President. I was looking forward to bringing all the states together and strengthening the Union, but one night in a theater in Washington, D.C., I was shot by a half-crazed actor. I died the next day.

I am considered one of America's greatest presidents.

Who was I?

JAMES POLK (1795-1849)

I was born in 1795 in North Carolina. As a youth I was a sickly boy. I graduated from the University of North Carolina with top honors in mathematics and the classics.

After serving in the Tennessee House of Representatives, I was sent to Congress where I served seven terms. At the age of forty-four I became the governor of Tennessee. In 1845 I became the eleventh President of the United States.

I carried out my program for the country in one term. Among my objectives was the acquisition of California, which I attained. Claiming that Mexico had invaded American territory, I declared war against Mexico. Many people felt that I had begun the war unnecessarily and unconstitutionally. I was greatly admired by my friends, but I never lived down my unpopularity with North-erners opposed to slavery.

Historian George Bancroft considered me "one of the very best, most honest, and most successful presidents the country ever had."

Who was I?

THEODORE ROOSEVELT (1858-1919)

I was born in New York City in 1858 to a family of wealth. I was a sickly child and was taught at home because I was not well enough to go to school. I worked in a gymnasium to build up my body. By the time I was ready to attend college, my health had improved enough that I was able to go.

Later I was elected to the New York State Legislature. In 1897 I became assistant secretary of the Navy. During the Spanish-American War, I left my job and gathered a group of soldiers to fight in Cuba. The soldiers were called Rough Riders. After leading my Rough Riders into battle up San Juan Hill, I became a national hero.

I served as governor of New York, Vice President of the United States, and President of the United States. As President I worked for conservation of our trees. I had the Panama Canal built. I broke up monopolies and sponsored laws for healthy food and workers' compensation. I helped establish our national parks. I believed in a strong military.

One of my famous remarks was "Speak softly and carry a big stick."

I was a man of adventure. I traveled in Africa, Europe, and South America. I was a rancher, a soldier, a big-game hunter, and one of America's best-loved presidents.

Who was I?

GEORGE WASHINGTON (1732-1799)

I was born in Virginia on February 22, 1732. During my youth I lived on a plantation and spent much time outside. Later I became a surveyor.

During the French and Indian War I was an Army commander. Several times I nearly lost my life. In one battle my coat showed four bullet holes. Two horses were shot from under me. Several years later, because of poor health, I retired to my home, Mount Vernon.

Sometime thereafter I returned to the Army as commander-in-chief and led the colonists against the British in the Revolutionary War. One winter my troops and I camped at Valley Forge, where we experienced terrible hardships. We did not have enough food or proper clothing. Many soldiers' feet froze and bled. Sickness spread, and many men died.

After we won the Revolutionary War, I was elected first President of the United States. The capital of our county, Washington, D.C., is named for me.

It is said that I was first in war, first in peace, and first in the hearts of my countrymen.

Who was I?

V
Famous Composers

Illustrated by
Harvey H. Lively

Use of the Puppets

Teacher/Librarian Use

Some ways of using the Famous Composers puppets are as follows:

1. To introduce a unit, biography, or musical piece
2. To review famous composers covered in the music or social studies curriculum
3. To culminate a unit in which famous composers figure prominently
4. To enrich a bulletin board display of student reports or a display of book jackets about famous composers

Student Use

Students may research, make, and present the puppets.

Recreational Use

The puppets may be used in recreational settings, such as at camp, at home, etc.

Johann Sebastian Bach

Ludwig Van Beethoven

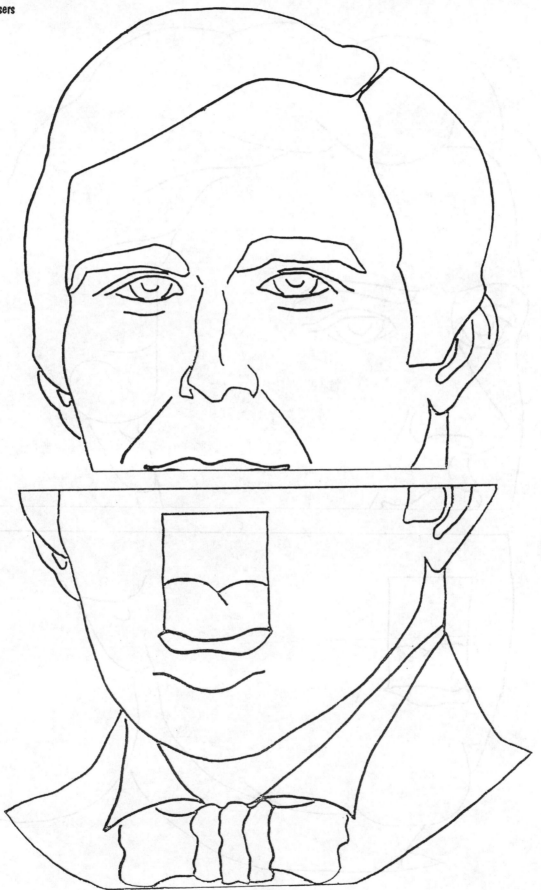

Stephen Foster

Wolfgang Amadeus Mozart

Riddles to Use with the Puppets

These riddles, which provide basic biographical information, may be told by either the instructor or by the students. If students are presenting the puppets, the instructor may let the students use the riddles in this book or may choose to have students do research and make up their own riddles. In a presentation, the puppet's name is withheld. The manipulator tells a riddle and at the conclusion chooses a student to identify the puppet.

JOHANN SEBASTIAN BACH (1685-1750)

I was born in Germany in 1685. Before I was ten years old my parents died, and I moved in with my older brother. In 1703 I joined an orchestra as a violinist. Later I became a church organist and composer.

My works were dominated by my deep religious feelings. I felt that religion was the basis of man's action and beliefs. Most amazingly, I was able to write hundreds of compositions in addition to supporting a very large family and fulfilling my duties as a musician and conductor. My complete works fill about sixty volumes.

In my time, I was appreciated as an organist. I was ignored as a composer, and only nine or ten of my works were published in my lifetime. My reputation as a composer was established seventy-nine years after my death by Felix Mendelssohn.

I was considered the greatest genius of baroque music.
Who was I?

LUDWIG VAN BEETHOVEN (1770-1827)

I was born in Germany in 1770. My childhood, an unhappy one, was spent in poverty. When I was very young my father taught me to play the piano and the violin, so I could help support our family. Soon I was composing.

My musical talents made me welcome at any musical gathering, thereby giving me an opportunity to meet important people. I had no trouble obtaining patrons and students.

People listened to my musical compositions for their own sake. Previously music was written for religious services, to teach, and to entertain. I made music more independent. I won a freedom for composers that they hadn't had before.

In the 1790s I began to lose my hearing. My personality changed and I became suspicious and irritable. When I became totally deaf, my social life suffered greatly. My composing was not affected.

My fifth and ninth symphonies are among my most famous works. I was one of the greatest composers in musical history.
Who was I?

STEPHEN FOSTER (1826-1864)

The youngest of nine children, I was born in Pittsburgh, Pennsylvania, on the Fourth of July, 1826. Music was an important part of the happy family to which I was born. By the time I was two, I began plucking tunes from a guitar. When I was ten, my uncle, who was very impressed with my musical ability, said I would be a famous man if I lived long enough.

By the time I was twenty, I had published a large number of songs. The publication of "Oh, Susanna" was an immediate success, but it, as my other songs, earned little money for me.

Shortly after my marriage at age twenty-four, I wrote some of my best-loved songs: "Jeanie with the Light Brown Hair," "Old Folks at Home," and others.

I was one of the best-loved and well-known composers in the country, and there is hardly an American who does not know some of my music.

Who was I?

WOLFGANG AMADEUS MOZART (1756-1791)

I was born in Austria in 1756. By the age of four I could play the harpsichord. At five I was composing music. At six I played for the Austrian empress. I never attended school. My father personally devoted himself to my general and musical education. I composed, played the organ, and toured Europe giving concerts.

I was skilled in almost every type of musical composition. I wrote twenty-two operas, over forty symphonies, a great amount of church music, serenades, concertos, chamber music, and sonatas. I helped popularize a new instrument of my time: the piano.

Although I tried to make a living composing, performing, and giving music lessons, I was unsuccessful. I died penniless in December 1791. Although I was only thirty-five when I died, I left over six hundred works.

I was one of the world's greatest composers.

Who was I?

VI
Folk Heroes

Illustrated by
Geraldine Hulbert

The Use of the Puppets

Teacher/Librarian Use

Some ways of using folk hero paper bag puppets are as follows:

1. To introduce a unit or research
2. To review folk heroes covered in the social studies or English curriculum
3. To culminate a unit in which folk heroes are prominent
4. To feature a folk hero in relation to a specific event
   - Arbor Day—After discussing Arbor Day, you might say something like this: "One of our most famous folk heroes went across America planting trees. I'm going to have him tell you about himself." (Present the Johnny Appleseed puppet and biographical material. If students are likely to identify the puppet, end with "Who Was I?" If not, end with "My name was Johnny Appleseed.")
   - Black History Month—After discussing the meaning of Black History Month, you might say something like this: "I'm going to tell you a riddle about a famous black folk hero. See if you can guess his name." (Present the John Henry puppet and the biographical riddle. If students are likely to identify the puppet, end with "Who was I?" If not, end by saying, "My name was John Henry.")
5. To enrich a bulletin board display of student reports or a display of book jackets about African Americans or folk heroes

Student Use

Students may research, make, and present the puppets.

Recreational Use

The puppets may be used in recreational settings, such as at camp or at home.

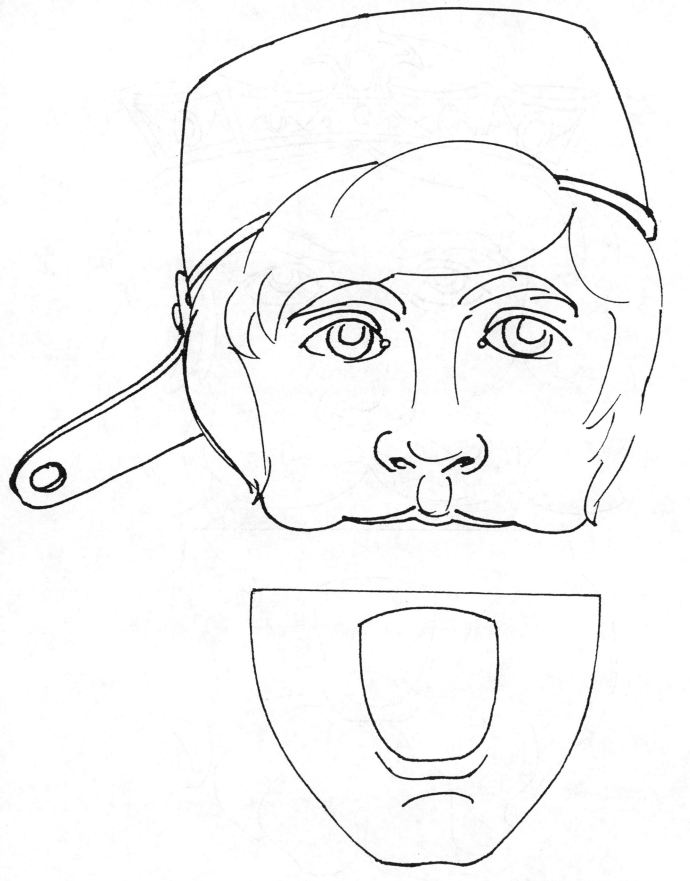

Johnny Appleseed

King Arthur

Daniel Boone

Paul Bunyan

Davy Crockett

Mike Fink

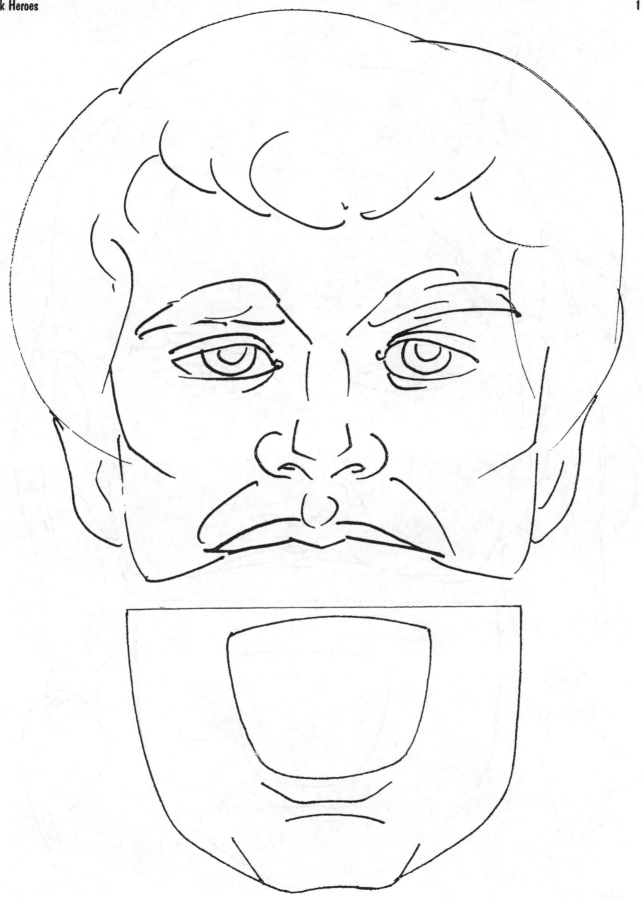

John Henry

Hiawatha

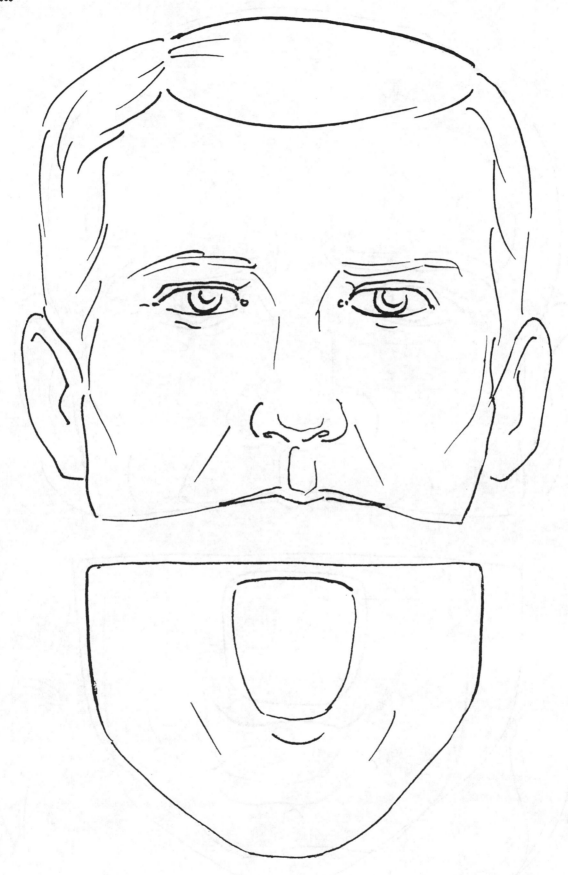

Casey Jones

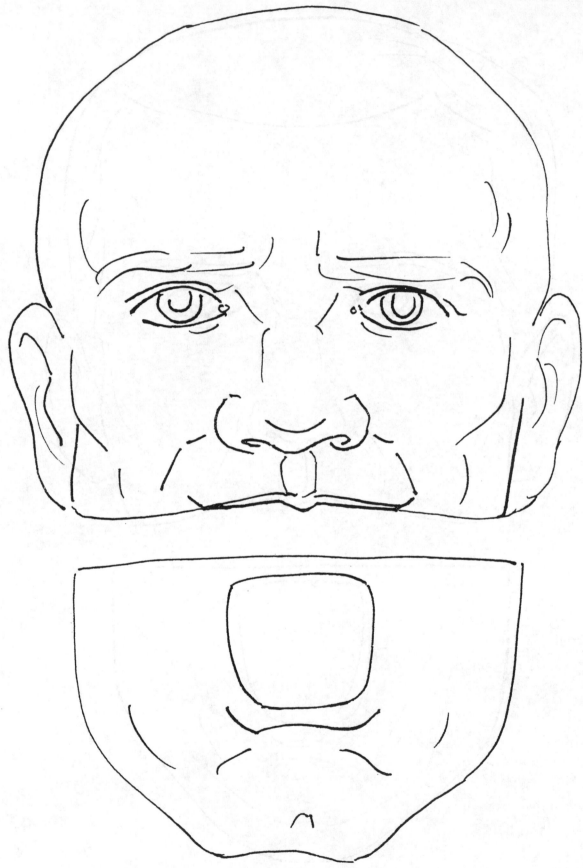

Joe Magarac

Pecos Bill

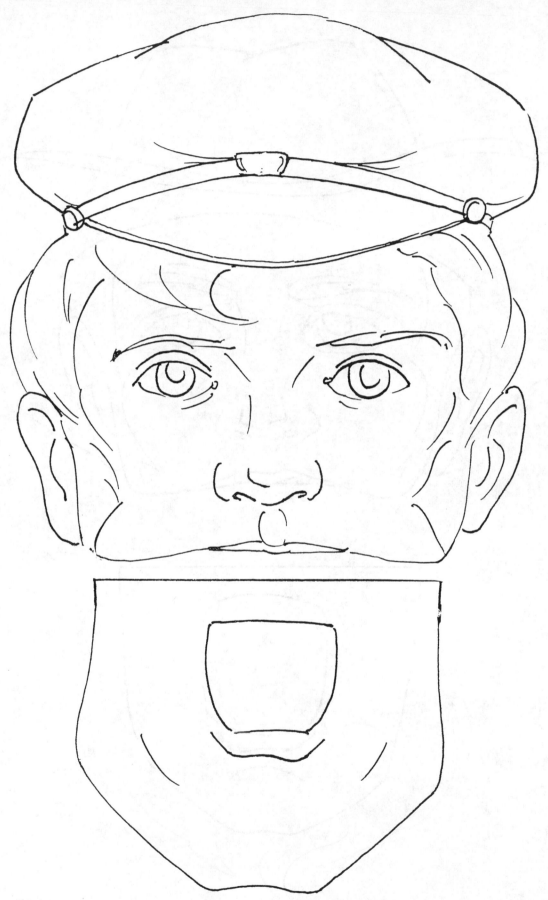

Stormalong

William Tell

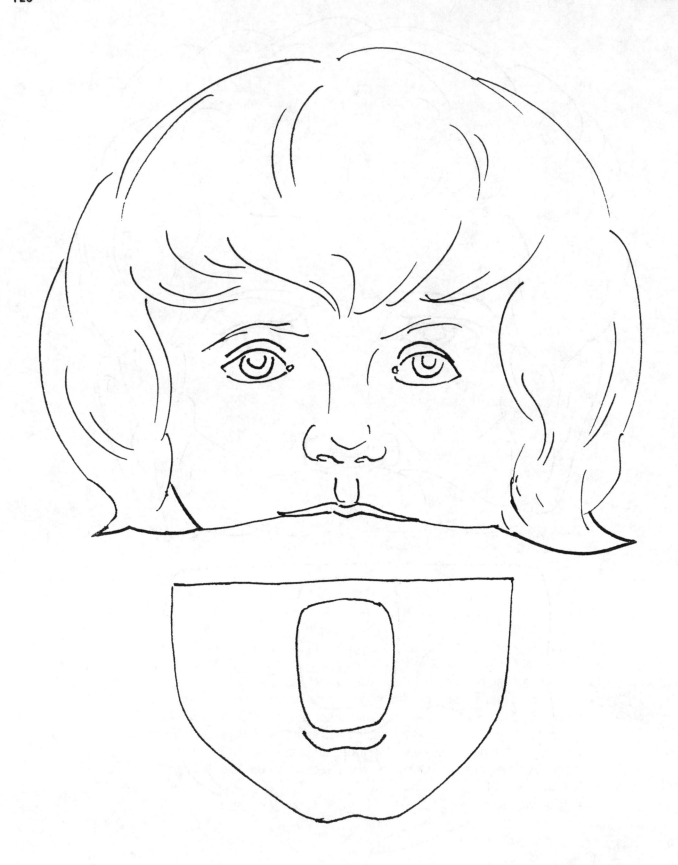

Dick Whittington

Riddles to Use with the Puppets

These riddles, which provide basic biographical information, may be told by either the instructor or by the students. If students are presenting the puppets, the instructor may let the students use the riddles in this book or may choose to have students do research and make up their own riddles. In a presentation, the puppet's name is withheld. The manipulator tells a riddle and at the conclusion chooses a student to identify the puppet.

JOHNNY APPLESEED (1774-1845)

I was born in Massachusetts in 1774. My parents named me Jonathan Chapman, but you know me by another name. As a young man, I worried that settlers moving west might not have enough food. I decided to plant apple trees across America to help them. For forty years I walked through the wilderness planting and tending to apple trees.

I wore a coffee sack for clothes. Because I had to carry a kettle for cooking, I wore my kettle as a hat. I carried a Bible under my arm and a bag of apple seeds over my shoulder. I had no knife or gun. I loved all living things and would never hurt any of them.

Once I freed a wolf that was caught in a trap. The wolf followed me like a dog for years. Another time when I noticed that bugs were being drawn into my campfire and burned, I put out the campfire.

I became a hero because of my great kindness to men and to animals.

Who was I?

KING ARTHUR (500 A.D.?-?)

I was one of the most famous heroes in medieval literature. History says I was probably a military chieftain living in Britain about A.D. 500. Legend says I was a king reigning at Camelot.

According to legend, the man who was able to remove a great sword stuck in a rock would become the next king. Although all the nobles had failed in their attempts to remove the sword, I succeeded. Actually I was the deceased king's son, who had been hidden away since birth.

As king, I gathered the bravest knights at my court. We sat at a Round Table so we could all be equal. With my wife Guinevere at my side, I brought order and peace to my kingdom. Once while I was away on an expedition, Mordred, my nephew, staged a rebellion. I returned and killed him, but I was seriously wounded. Thereafter, I was carried away secretly to the Isle of Avalon to be healed.

Who was I?

DANIEL BOONE (1734-1820)

I was an American pioneer and backwoodsman, born in 1734. I knew my way in the woods so well that the Indians thought I had magic powers. Once when they surrounded me, I ran through the forest this way and that, trying to cover my tracks. Suddenly my tracks and I disappeared. The Indians thought a spirit had led them on the chase, so they returned to their war party. I had saved myself by swinging up into a tree on a wild grapevine.

Once I cut three notches in the bark of an ash tree to show where I had spent the night. Twenty years later some men were trying to locate the boundary of a piece of land. All they knew about the location was that the boundary began with an ash tree marked with three notches of a white man's tomahawk. Although I had put lots of notches in trees in twenty years, I was able to find the tree.

I was a real person, a famous frontier hero, but I was also a person about whom many a tall tale was told.

Who was I?

PAUL BUNYAN

According to American folklore, I was a giant lumberjack who dug the Grand Canyon. My constant companion was a huge blue ox named Babe. Babe was so large that a crow that usually roosted on Babe's left horn tried to fly to the right horn one winter. By the next spring it lighted on the other horn.

I only had 14,000 men at my logging camp because I didn't like crowds. My bunkhouse was so tall that the last seven stories had to be put on hinges to let the moon go by. One time I had a fight with Big Swede. After the battle, all that remained of the mountain where we fought was a small pile of earth. Today that place is called the Bad Lands of the Dakotas.

Before I changed America there were no mountains, lakes, or rivers. There was only flat land. Everywhere I went things changed.

Who was I?

DAVY CROCKETT (1786-1836)

I was one of the most famous frontiersman of history, legend, and folklore. I was born in Tennessee in 1786. In 1813 I became a scout for the U.S. Army. Later I was elected to the U.S. House of Representatives three times. My motto was "Be always sure you're right—then go ahead!"

Known for my ability to exaggerate, I told many a tall tale. One was about how I freed the sun when it got caught between two cakes of ice. Another was about how I got a raccoon to give up by grinning at him.

I was a hunter, Indian fighter, and hero who fought and died at the Alamo. Who was I?

MIKE FINK (1770-1823)

I was an American frontiersman and boatman, born in 1770. I was an expert shot. According to legend I never lost a shooting contest. I had my first rifle at twelve, at thirteen I fought Indians, and at seventeen I became an Indian scout.

For twenty years I worked on keelboats and earned a reputation for strength and skill. When the steamboat began to replace the keelboat, I became a hunter and trapper.

One time Davy Crockett challenged me to a shooting match. We proved to be evenly matched at snuffing out candles, driving nails, and shooting flies from a cow's horn. When I shot half a comb from my wife's head, Davy refused to shoot. I won the match.

Shooting tin cups off the heads of friends was one of the things we did for fun in those days. Once I shot at a cup on a friend's head, missed, and killed my friend. I myself was shot dead by an avenger (someone who wanted revenge).

Who was I?

JOHN HENRY

According to American folklore, I was a Black steel-driving champion. When I was born I weighed forty-four pounds. After my first meal, I went out looking for work. I got a job at the C & O Railroad laying tracks and driving tunnels.

Some railroads were using steam drills by then, but the C & O still used men. One day my foreman decided to have a contest to see if a man could drive a hole deeper into a rock than a steam drill could. He offered a $100 prize. I stepped up and said I could drive deeper than a steam drill could.

On the day of the contest, I picked up two large hand hammers and swung them with a mighty force over and over and over again. The steam drill drilled and drilled. I dug two holes seven feet deep. The steam drill drilled one hole nine feet deep. I won, but all my hammering caused a blood vessel to burst, and I died that night.

Who was I?

HIAWATHA

I was the legendary Indian folk hero in a poem by Henry Wadsworth Longfellow.

My grandmother, Nokomis, raised me by the shores of Gitche Gumee. As a youth I learned the names, languages, and secrets of all the animals in the forest. I also gained the wisdom and magic powers I needed to take revenge against my father, the West Wind, for his treatment of my mother.

When Grandmother Nokomis told me that a wicked magician, Pearl-Feather, had killed her father and sent fever and disease to our people, I took my bow and killed him. I became the leader of my tribe, and I foretold the coming of white people. The beautiful Minnehaha became my wife.

I was an Indian hero who was admired not only for my wisdom and courage, but most importantly for my goodness.

Who was I?

CASEY JONES (1863-1900)

I was born in Kentucky in 1863. My real name was John Luther Jones. When I was twenty-six, I became an engineer for an Illinois train named Cannonball. I was a very skillful engineer, and I always brought my train in on time.

One night when I finished bringing the Cannonball in, I heard that the engineer of another train was ill and couldn't make his run. I volunteered to make the run even though the train was already one hour and thirty-six minutes late. I was determined to make up the time. I would have if I hadn't suddenly come upon a stalled train on the track. Being faced with a life-and-death situation, I told the fireman to jump, and he did. I stayed with the train and saved my passengers and crew, but I died in the performance of my duty. My body was found with one hand on the whistle cord and one on the air-brake lever.

My Negro engine wiper, Wallace Saunders, wrote a ballad about me. It is one of the most familiar songs in America's folklore.

Who was I?

JOE MAGARAC (MAG uh rak)

According to American folklore, I was a hero of the steel mills. I first became well-known for winning a strong-man contest at a Fourth of July picnic.

Later I got a job in the steel mill and worked night and day. I never slept or rested. I stirred, scooped, and poured steel. I made cannonballs with my bare hands. I squeezed railroad rails from between my fingers.

One day the boss found me sitting in the ladle with the steel bubbling up around my neck. I said that I had heard that the finest steel in the world was needed to build a new mill and I was going to give myself for that purpose. I was the finest steel.

Steel workers remember me proudly.

Who was I?

PECOS BILL

According to American folklore, I was born in Texas. When my folks headed west in the family wagon, I fell out. There were so many children in my family that I wasn't missed for several days. By then it was too late for my folks to turn back to look for me. I was raised by coyotes. I thought I was a coyote until one day I found out that I didn't have a tail.

When I grew up I became a cowboy. One time, using a rattlesnake for a whip, I mounted a mountain lion and rode him all over the countryside.

You may have wondered how the Rio Grande River came to be. I dug it during a dry spell to get water from the Gulf of Mexico.

I was a mythical super-cowboy. I invented roping and other cowboy skills. I had two loves: my horse Widow-Maker and my gal Slue-Foot Sue.

Who was I?

STORMALONG

According to American folklore, I was the hero of sailors' tall tales. By the time I was ten years old I was twelve feet tall. At thirteen I signed on a ship as a cabin boy. I had to sleep in an extra-large lifeboat, as that was the only thing large enough to hold me. For breakfast I could eat a boatload of eggs, plus all the hens who laid them.

When I grew up I couldn't find a ship big enough for me, so I got a few thousand shipyard workers to help me build one. It took three years to finish it. We used so much wood that we caused a lumber shortage throughout the entire country. The masts were so tall they scraped the moon and sun.

I was a giant sailor about whom many a tall tale was told.

Who was I?

WILLIAM TELL

I was a legendary hero of Switzerland.

In 1307 all men were required to pay reverence to an invading governor's hat, which was placed on a pole. I did not pay reverence to the hat. The penalty for failing to honor the governor's hat was the loss of one's life and one's property. However, the governor gave me a chance to save my life. I was to shoot an apple off my son's head at one hundred paces. If I succeeded, I would go free. If I missed, I would die. I succeeded.

Later when the governor kicked his horse forward in an attempt to trample a woman and her children, I shot an arrow and killed him. Afterwards the people rose up and threw the invaders out. They declared that I was the savior of Switzerland.

My historical existence has been disputed. Did I really live? I'll leave that question for you to answer.

Who was I?

DICK WHITTINGTON (1358?-1423)

According to history I was born in England about 1358. After becoming an orphan, a kind London merchant hired me to work in his kitchen. The merchant, who was sending a ship overseas, expected each of his servants to send something to be sold. I reluctantly sent my only possession: my cat.

In a storm, the trading ship was driven to the coast of Barbary, where the king, plagued by mice and rats, paid a fortune for my cat.

Meanwhile I had run away to escape the cook, who constantly mistreated me. As I trudged along, I heard some church bells which seemed to say that I would become Lord Mayor of London. I decided that if I were to become Lord Mayor, I'd go back.

On arriving in London, I collected the fortune from the sale of my cat, which made me very rich. Thereafter I married the merchant's daughter and became Lord Mayor of London three times.

Who was I?

VII
Storybook Puppets

Illustrated by
Carol Ditter Waters

Use of the Puppets

Teacher/Librarian Use

Some ways Storybook Puppets can be used are as follows:

1. To introduce a book. For example, in introducing *Snow White*, the instructor might present the Snow White puppet and have it say something like this: "My stepmother was an evil queen who was so jealous of my beauty that she ordered a servant to kill me. Listen as the teacher/librarian reads a book about what happened to me."
2. To follow up the reading of a story. For example, a week or longer after reading a story, the instructor may want to present a follow-up riddle. If so, use the puppet to tell the riddle. Then call on a student to give the answer.
3. To enrich a bulletin board display of student work or a display of book jackets

Student Use

Students may be asked to make storybook puppets. They may or may not be required to present brief riddles also. Students' puppets may be displayed on a bulletin board or on a clothesline strung across the classroom.

Recreational Use

Storybook puppets may be used in recreational settings, such as at camp or at home.

Cinderella's head

Cinderella's body

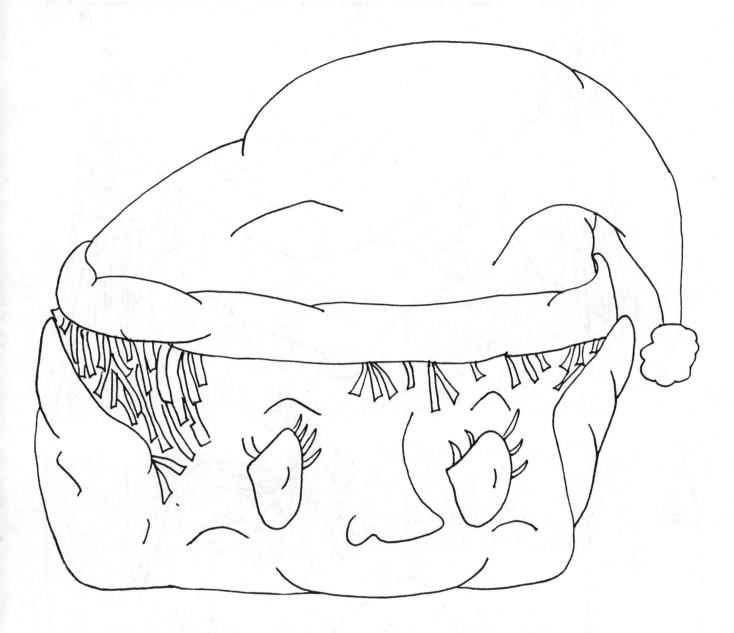

Elf's head

Elf's body

Goldilocks's head

Goldilocks's body

Bear's head

Bear's body

Hansel's head

Hansel's body

Gretel's head

Gretel's body

Jack's head

Jack's body

Little Red Riding Hood's head

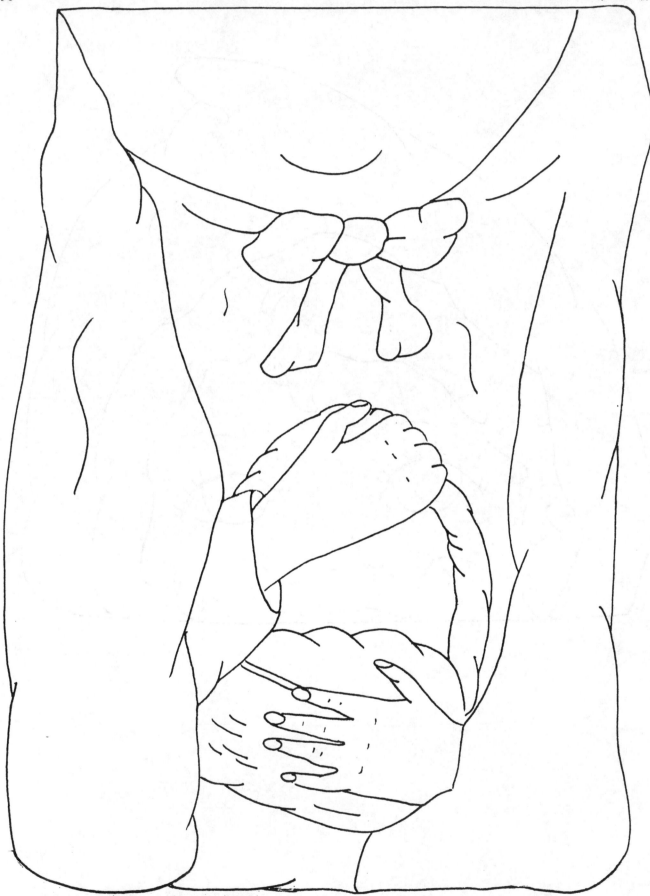

Little Red Riding Hood's body

Pied Piper's head

Pied Piper's body

Puss in Boots's head

154

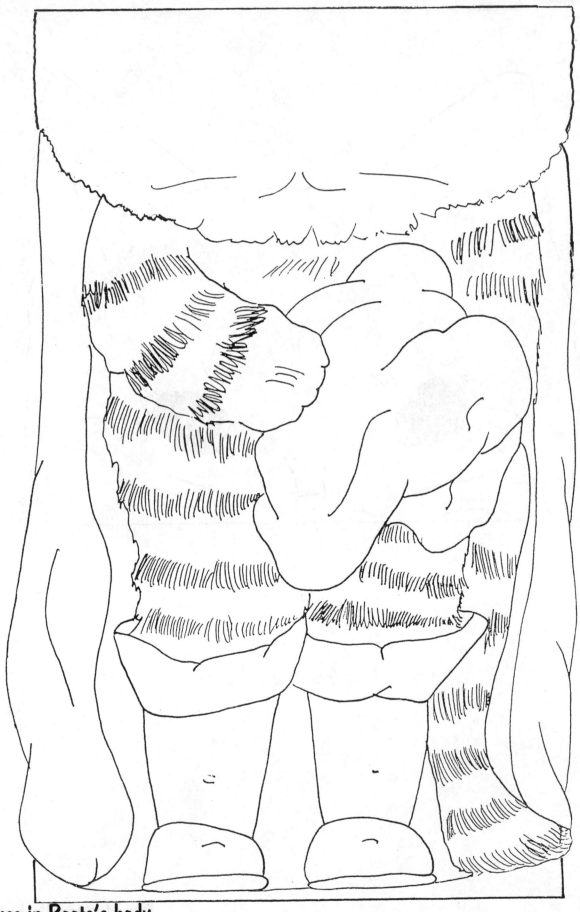

Puss in Boots's body

Rapunzel's head

Rapunzel's body

Rumpelstiltskin's head

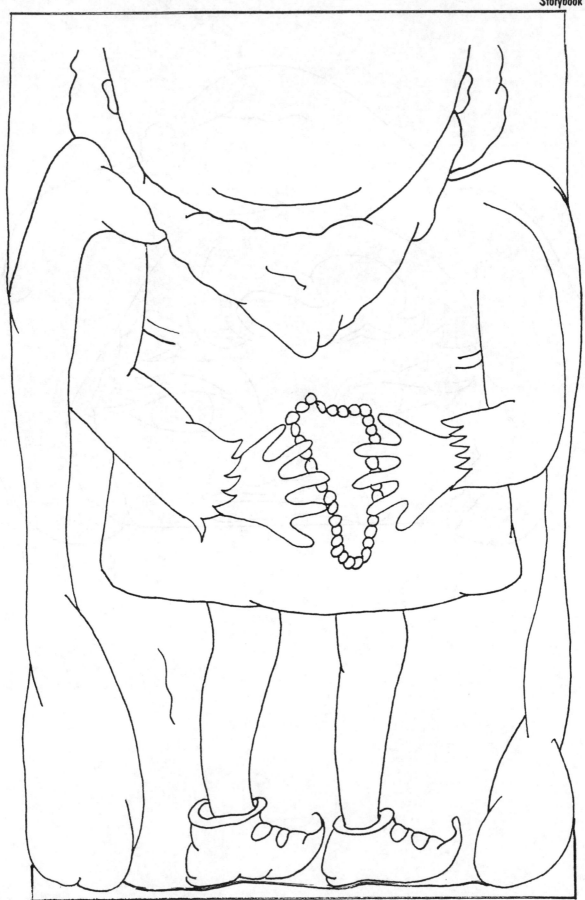

Rumpelstiltskin's body

Sleeping Beauty's head

Sleeping Beauty's body

Snow White's head

Snow White's body

Goat's head

Goat's body

Pig's head

Pig's body

Riddles to Use with the Puppets

For each of the following stories there are two riddles: a long one and a mini-one. Choose the one you prefer.

Begin by reading a storybook or telling a story to your students. In about a week or so, tell a riddle—long or mini—about the story you presented. A variation would be to present long riddles a week after a storybook is read and use mini-riddles as a culmination to a whole series of storybook readings. As a culmination, a number of mini-riddles would be presented at one time.

You might begin a presentation with something like this: "I'm going to tell a riddle to you. Listen and see if you know who the riddle is about. Don't speak out. At the end of the riddle, if you know the answer, raise your hand. I'll call on someone to answer."

Bring the puppet out and let it tell the riddle.

CINDERELLA

My cruel stepmother and stepsisters gave me only rags to wear and made me work all the time. When the king's son gave a ball, my stepsisters dressed in beautiful silks and attended in style. As I sat crying because I couldn't attend, my fairy godmother appeared. She told me I could go to the ball, but she said I must not stay after midnight. Then she turned a pumpkin into a fine coach, six mice into horses, a rat into a coachman, and six lizards into six footmen. Waving her wand, she turned my rags into a beautiful ball gown and my shoes into a pair of glass slippers.

At the ball, the prince danced with me until the stroke of midnight, at which time I fled leaving behind a glass slipper. In his effort to find me, the prince proclaimed that the woman whose foot would fit into the glass slipper would become his wife.

When the prince came to my house, he found that the glass slipper didn't fit my stepsisters. However, when he tried the slipper on my foot, it fit perfectly. I quickly pulled the other slipper from my pocket and put it on. The prince was overjoyed. He took me to his palace where we married and where we lived happily for the rest of our days.

Who was I?

Mini-riddle

My fairy godmother turned my rags into silks and made it possible for me to attend a ball in style. Although I lost a glass slipper, a prince found me, returned the slipper, and made me his wife.

THE ELVES AND THE SHOEMAKER

A very poor shoemaker had only enough leather to make one pair of shoes. One night he cut the leather out and left it on a table to work on in the morning.

The next day the shoemaker found that the shoes had been made during the night. Soon the shoes were sold and the shoemaker bought enough leather for two pairs of shoes. That night the shoemaker cut the shoes out, and the next morning he found that they were finished. He quickly sold them and bought leather for four pairs of shoes. At night he cut shoes out, and the next morning he found them finished. This continued until the shoemaker had become very rich.

One day he said to his wife, "Let's stay up tonight and see who is making the shoes." That night the shoemaker and his wife hid and waited. At midnight my brother and I came in and quickly made the shoes. The next day the shoemaker's wife said, "Those two little elves have made us rich. Poor things they have no clothes. Let's show them we are grateful by making them some shirts, pants, and shoes." The shoemaker agreed. That night after making tiny clothes for us, they left them on the table and hid and waited.

At midnight when my brother and I arrived, we were surprised and delighted to find the clothes. After dressing, we danced off into the night and were never seen again. As for the shoemaker and his wife, they lived well and happily for the rest of their lives.

Which fairy tale tells our story?

Mini-riddle

My brother and I stitched leather into shoes for a shoemaker and his wife, thereby making them rich. In gratitude the shoemaker and his wife made some clothes for my brother and me.

Which fairy tale tells our story?

GOLDILOCKS AND THE THREE BEARS

Manipulate the Goldilocks puppet

Once when I was playing in the woods, I came upon a pretty little house. The door was open, so I went inside. In the kitchen, I found three bowls of porridge. I took a spoonful of the porridge from the big bowl. It was too hot. Then I took a spoonful from the middle-sized bowl. It was too cold. Then I took a spoonful from the little bowl. It was just right, so I ate all of it.

I looked for a chair to sit in. First I sat in a big chair, but it was too hard. Next I sat in a middle-sized chair, but it was too soft. Then I sat in a little chair. It was just right, but when I sat down the chair broke into pieces.

At the top of a flight of stairs, I found a bedroom with three beds. I lay down on the big bed. It was too hard. Next I lay down on the middle-sized bed. It was too soft. Then I lay down on the little bed. It was just right, and I fell asleep.

Put Goldilocks aside, and manipulate the bear puppet

My father, mother, and I had been out for a walk. When we returned, we sat down to eat. Papa Bear said, "Someone's been eating my porridge." Mama Bear said, "Someone's been eating my porridge." I said, "Someone's been eating my porridge and has eaten it all up." Papa Bear said, "Someone's been sitting in my chair." Mama Bear said, "Someone's been sitting in my chair." I said, "Someone's been sitting in my chair and has broken it into pieces."

We went upstairs to the bedroom. Papa Bear said, "Someone's been sleeping in my bed." Mama Bear said, "Someone's been sleeping in my bed." I said, "Someone's been sleeping in my bed, and there she is."

Put the bear aside, and manipulate the Goldilocks puppet

With all the noise, I woke up. When I saw the three bears looking down at me, I jumped up quickly and ran home as fast as I could. I never ever went into anyone's house uninvited again.

Who was I, and who did I meet in the house in the woods?

Mini-riddle

I entered an empty house uninvited, ate a bowl of porridge, broke a chair, and lay down on a bed and fell asleep. The family who lived in the house came home and scared me away.

Who was I, and whom did I meet in the house in the woods?

HANSEL AND GRETEL

Manipulate the Hansel puppet

Because my family was so poor, my stepmother urged my father to take my sister and me to the forest and leave us. As father led my sister and me into the forest, I dropped white pebbles along the path so my sister and I would be able to find our way back home. The second time father took us into the forest, I dropped bread crumbs to mark a trail. Sadly, when my sister and I started home, we found that the birds had eaten the crumbs.

After being lost for three days, we came upon a house made of gingerbread. The old woman who lived in the house invited us inside. At first she seemed nice, but she locked me in a cage and spent days trying to fatten me up so she could eat me.

Put the Hansel puppet aside, and manipulate the Gretel puppet

One day the witch told me to climb into the oven to see if it was hot. Realizing that the witch planned to push me in, I pushed her in instead. Then I let my brother out of his cage. My brother and I found a path through the forest that led us home. Our father, who said our stepmother had gone, was overjoyed to see us.

Thereafter, my brother and I lived happily together with our father.

Bring Hansel back and have both puppets speak

Who were we?

Mini-riddle

After being left in the woods, my brother and I happened upon a gingerbread house. The witch who lived there locked my brother in a cage and planned to eat him. She tried to push me into an oven, but I pushed her in instead.

Who were my brother and I?

JACK AND THE BEANSTALK

After I traded a cow for some magic beans, which my mother threw into the yard, a gigantic beanstalk sprouted up. At the top of the beanstalk, high in the sky, was an ogre's castle. One day I climbed up to the castle, and being very hungry, I asked the ogre's wife for some food. As I sat eating, the sound of thump, thump, thump echoed through the castle.

"My husband is returning," said the ogre's wife. "Quick, hide in the oven." As I hid in the oven, the ogre roared, "Fee-fi-fo-fum, I smell the blood of an Englishman. Be he alive, or be he dead, I'll grind his bones to make my bread."

The ogre's wife quickly put some food out for the ogre. As the ogre ate, he forgot his suspicions. When he finished eating, he told his wife to bring his two bags of gold to him. After the ogre counted the gold, he fell asleep. Climbing out of the oven, I grabbed a bag of gold and rushed down the beanstalk.

After mother and I spent the gold, I climbed the beanstalk again. This time the ogre had his wife bring his hen that laid golden eggs. As soon as the ogre fell asleep, I grabbed the hen and hurried down the beanstalk.

The last time I climbed the beanstalk, the ogre called for his magic harp. As the ogre fell asleep, I grabbed the harp and started down the beanstalk. Suddenly the ogre woke up and started chasing me. As I reached the bottom of the beanstalk, I yelled for my mother to bring an ax. Receiving it, I quickly chopped the beanstalk down, causing the mean, old ogre to fall to his death. With the magic harp and the hen that laid golden eggs to keep us happy, mother and I lived well for the rest of our days.

Which fairy tale tells my story?

Mini-riddle

I traded a cow for five magic beans, which sprouted into a gigantic beanstalk. At the top of the beanstalk lived a mean, old ogre. I fooled the ogre and took his gold, his harp, and his hen that laid golden eggs.

Which fairy tale tells my story?

LITTLE RED RIDING HOOD

One day as I was walking through the woods to Grandmother's house, I met a wolf. When the wolf asked me where I was going, I said I was taking a basket of goodies to my grandmother. As I walked on, the wolf turned around and ran to Grandmother's house along another path.

When the wolf arrived at Grandmother's, he entered, chased Grandmother, and then locked her in a closet. Afterwards he put on one of Grandmother's gowns and nightcaps and climbed into her bed.

When I reached Grandmother's and entered her bedroom, I was surprised at the face peering out from under the covers. A strange conversation took place.

"Grandmother, what big ears you have."

"All the better to hear you with, my dear."

"Grandmother, what big eyes you have."

"All the better to see you with, my dear."

"Grandmother, what big teeth you have."

"All the better to eat you with, my dear."

Then the wolf jumped out of the bed and began to chase me. I screamed and screamed as we went around and around. A woodcutter, hearing my cries, came bounding to my rescue and chased the wolf away.

Suddenly there was the sound of loud pounding coming from the closet. The woodcutter unlocked the closet door, and Grandmother stepped out. We were so happy that everyone was safe. We unpacked all the goodies I had brought, and then we sat down and had a wonderful party.

Who was I?

Mini-riddle

A wolf pretended to be my Grandmother by putting on Grandmother's gown and nightcap and climbing into her bed. When the wolf started after me, a woodcutter chased him away.

Who was I?

THE PIED PIPER OF HAMELIN

Hamelin was infested with rats. They were everywhere—in every barn, house, and storeroom. Not only did they eat everything, they squeaked and shrieked and made terrible noises.

One day when the mayor and town council were trying to figure out how to rid Hamelin of rats, I appeared. "What will you pay me if I get rid of every rat in Hamelin?" I asked. When it was agreed that I should be paid fifty pounds, I stepped out into the street and began to play my pipe. As I played, rats came running from everywhere, from holes, pantries, and cupboards. I walked up and down the streets playing my pipe with the rats following me. Finally, I led the rats out of town and into the ocean. It was there that they all drowned.

After I had rid Hamelin of its rats, I went to collect the fifty pounds I had been promised. The mayor and the council said they would pay only twenty pounds, not fifty. They wouldn't listen when I warned them I could pipe many kinds of tunes. I went out into the street and began playing my pipe. From everywhere children appeared, singing, dancing, following me. Through the streets we went, over hills and mountains, and into the dark woods until we disappeared. We were never seen again. From that day to this no one knows what happened to us.

Who was I?

Mini-riddle

I played my pipe and led all of the rats of Hamelin out of town, through the woods, and into the ocean, where they drowned. When I was not paid the amount of money I was promised, I played my pipe again and led all of Hamelin's children away, never to be seen again.

Who was I?

PUSS IN BOOTS

When a miller with three sons died, he left his mill to his first son, his donkey to his second son, and me to his third son. I told the third son if he would give me a pair of boots and a sack, he would find that I wasn't as useless as he thought.

After the son gave me some boots and a sack, I caught a rabbit and took it to the king and said that my master, the Marquis de Carabas, had sent it. That was the first of many such gifts. I told my master to bathe in the river and when he did, I shouted, "My master the Marquis de Carabas is drowning." The king, who was driving by with his daughter, dragged my master from the river, dressed him richly, and had him ride in his carriage. I ran ahead and told all the workers in the fields that if they were asked to whom this land belonged, they should say it belonged to the Marquis de Carabas. The king stopped several times and was always told the same thing. He decided the Marquis de Carabas must be very rich.

I hurried to a castle, which belonged to a wicked ogre. On seeing the ogre, I said, "I hear you can turn yourself into any animal you choose, but I won't believe it unless I see it for myself." The ogre turned himself into a lion. I said, "Can you turn yourself into something small—er—uh—perhaps a mouse?" When the ogre changed into a mouse, I quickly ate him.

As the king's carriage reached the castle, I said, "Welcome to the home of my master the Marquis de Carabas." The king thought, "What a rich man the Marquis must be." Soon the king consented to the marriage of his daughter to my master. Afterwards the princess, my master, and I moved into the castle, which had belonged to the ogre, and lived there happily ever after.

Mini-riddle

After tricking an ogre into turning himself into a mouse, I ate him and took his castle. I convinced a king that my poor master was rich and the king consented to letting my master marry his daughter.

Who was I?

RAPUNZEL

A witch, who caught my father taking lettuce from her garden, made him promise to give her his first child. Shortly after I was born, the witch came and took me. When I was twelve, the witch locked me in a tower, which had neither doors nor stairs, but which had one small window at the top. To get into the tower, the witch would call for me to let down my hair and she would climb up.

A prince, who had seen how the witch got into the tower, called out to me to let down my hair, and he climbed up. When the witch learned about the prince and his visits, she cut off my hair and took me to a desert and left me. The next time the prince came, the witch put down the hair and the prince climbed up. When the witch told him that he'd never see me again, he jumped from the tower and was blinded by some thorns.

For a year, the blind prince wandered about until one day he happened upon the desert, where I was. When I saw him, I put my arms around him and wept. Two of my tears fell into his eyes and healed them. Overjoyed at our good fortune, the prince and I journeyed to his kingdom, where we married and lived happily ever after.

Who was I?

Mini-riddle

A witch entered a tower, where she had locked me, by climbing up my hair. After the witch took me to a desert, she tricked a prince into the tower and made him fall and become blinded. When the prince found me, my tears healed his blindness.

Who was I?

RUMPELSTILTSKIN

A poor miller told a king that he had a daughter who was not only beautiful, but that she could spin straw into gold. The king said that if that was true, he would make the daughter his queen. To determine the truth of the claim, the king had the daughter brought to the palace and locked in a room full of straw. The king told the miller's daughter that if the straw wasn't spun into gold by the next morning, she would die.

While the girl was crying, I entered. When the girl said she would give me her necklace if I would spin the straw into gold, I agreed. The second time the girl was left to spin, she promised the ring on her finger if I would spin the straw into gold. The third time, the girl promised that when she became queen she would give me her first child. Again I agreed and spun the straw into gold.

After the girl became queen and gave birth, she begged me to let her keep the child. I told her that I would give her three days to guess my name. If she could guess it in that time she could keep her child. On the first two days, the queen failed to guess my name, but on the third day she succeeded. I was so upset that the queen had guessed my name that I raged and screamed and finally tore myself in two.

Who was I?

Mini-riddle

I spun straw into gold for a miller's daughter. When the daughter became queen, I told her I would release her from her promise to give me her first child if she could guess my name.

Who was I?

SLEEPING BEAUTY

All seven fairies who lived in my parents' kingdom were invited to my christening. As everyone was sitting down, a very old fairy, who hadn't been seen for years and years, appeared. After six of the fairies gave gifts to me, the old fairy stepped forward. She said I would pierce my hand on a spindle and die. The seventh fairy said she couldn't undo what the old fairy had done, but she said I wouldn't die; instead I would fall asleep for a hundred years and then a prince would come and wake me. When I was sixteen, I did prick my hand on a spindle and fall asleep. The seventh fairy came and put everyone in the palace to sleep so they would not awaken before me.

A hundred years later a prince came upon the palace, which was hidden by an overgrowth of trees and bushes. After an old man told the prince about the uninvited fairy's spell, the prince made his way through the brambles and into the palace. There he found everyone asleep, as they had been for one hundred years. When the prince came to where I lay, he kissed me. At that moment I awakened, as did everyone in the palace.

Life went on in the castle as it had a hundred years before. It was as if nothing had happened. In a short time, I married the prince and we lived happily the rest of our lives.

Who was I?

Mini-riddle

I pricked my hand on a spindle and fell asleep for a hundred years. After being kissed by a prince, I woke up.

Who was I?

SNOW WHITE AND THE SEVEN DWARFS

My stepmother was an evil queen who became very jealous every time she looked into a magic mirror, which told her I was more beautiful than she.

One day the queen ordered a servant to take me to the forest and kill me. The servant took pity on me, and when we got into the forest, he told me to run away. I wandered through the forest until I came to a little house. No one was home, so I went inside, lay down, and took a nap. At the time I didn't know it, but the house belonged to seven dwarfs. When the dwarfs came home from working in the mines, they listened to my story. They asked me to stay with them, and I did.

The queen's mirror told her that I was alive and living at the dwarfs' house. Disguising herself as a peddler, the queen tried to kill me three times. The last time she tricked me into biting a poisoned apple, which put me into a deep sleep. Thinking I was dead, the dwarfs placed me in a glass coffin.

One day a prince, who was riding by, stopped, came to the coffin, and kissed me. I awakened. Thereafter, the prince and I fell in love and were to be married. It happened that my stepmother was invited to the wedding. When she recognized me, she became so angry that she fell down and had to be taken home. She died soon thereafter. As for the prince and I, we married and lived long and happy lives.

Who was I?

Mini-riddle

My stepmother, who was jealous of my beauty, gave me a poisoned apple, which put me into a deep sleep. A prince, seeing me lie in a glass coffin, kissed me, and I awakened.

Who was I?

THE THREE BILLY GOATS GRUFF

My two brothers and I lived on a mountainside where there was very little to eat. Not far from our home was a beautiful pasture of green grass, but to get to the pasture we had to pass over a bridge. Under the bridge lived a big, bad troll.

One day my youngest brother started over the bridge. Trip-trap, trip-trap. The troll, who heard my brother, began to roar, "Who trips over my bridge?"

"It is only I," said my youngest brother.

"I'm going to eat you," said the troll.

"Please don't eat me. My older brother is coming, and he's bigger than I am."

The troll was very hungry and a larger meal sounded good. "Very well," said the troll, and he let my brother pass.

My second brother started over the bridge. Trip-trap, trip-trap.

"Who's tripping over my bridge?" the troll roared.

"It is I," said my second brother.

"I'm going to eat you," roared the troll.

"Please don't eat me. My bigger brother is coming soon. He is much larger than I."

"Even larger," thought the troll. "Very well." And he let my second brother pass.

Soon I started to cross the bridge. Trip-trap, trip-trap.

"Who is tripping over my bridge?" roared the troll.

"It is I," I replied.

"I'm going to come up and eat you," roared the troll.

"Come ahead," I said.

As the troll approached, I put down my head and rushed forward.

Catching him with my horns, I hurled him off the bridge and into the deep water flowing below. He screamed and splashed and then sank from view. From that day to this, no one has ever seen the troll again.

As for my two brothers and me, we continued to live on the mountainside, but whenever we were hungry, we crossed the bridge to the pasture and ate until we were full.

Who were we?

Mini-riddle

My two brothers and I wanted to cross a bridge so we could eat in a green pasture on the other side. After the troll, who lived beneath the bridge, threatened each of us, I pushed him over the side of the bridge and into the water.

Who were my brothers and I?

THE THREE LITTLE PIGS

One day my two brothers and I set off to build strong homes to protect us from the big, bad wolf. My first brother built a house of straw. My second brother built a house of sticks. I built a house of bricks.

One day the big, bad wolf went to my brother's house of straw and said, "Little pig, little pig, let me come in." My brother said, "No, no, not by the hair of my chinny-chin-chin. I won't let you in." The wolf said, "Then I'll huff and puff and I'll blow your house in." And the wolf huffed and puffed, and he blew the house in and ate my brother.

Sometime later the wolf went to my second brother's house—to the house made of sticks. The same thing happened to my second brother that happened to my first brother.

One day the wolf came to my house of bricks. Although the wolf huffed and puffed, he couldn't blow my house in. Twice the wolf tried to lure me from my house. Once by telling me he'd show me where to find some fine turnips. The second time by telling me he'd show me where to find some delicious apples. I outstmarted him both times. When the wolf told me he'd meet me at the fair, I bought a butter churn and rolled home.

Desperate, the wolf climbed up to my roof and started to come down my chimney. Again I outsmarted him. I built a fire and put a big pot over it. When the wolf slid down the chimney, he fell into the pot. That was the end of the big, bad wolf.

My two brothers and I tried to build homes to protect ourselves from the wolf. Who were we?

Mini-riddle

One of my brothers built a house of straw, another a house of sticks, and I built a house of bricks. After much huffing and puffing, a wolf blew down the house of straw and the house of sticks, but he couldn't blow down my house of bricks.

Who were my brothers and I?

VIII
Halloween Puppets

Illustrated by
Carol Ditter Waters

Use of the Puppets

Teacher/Librarian Use

Some ways of using Halloween puppets are as follows:

1. To make a holiday announcement
   - Have one of the puppets announce the Halloween school parade/activities.
   - Use a puppet to present some Halloween safety rules.
   - Let a puppet introduce a Halloween song the class is going to learn.
2. To present a holiday greeting
   - Have the witch greet the children. She might screech out something like this: "Heh, heh, heh, heh! Happy Halloween, boys and girls. Tonight (tomorrow/ _____) is Halloween. I'll be swooping down over (name of city), and I'll be looking for you. Watch for me. Happy Halloween. Heh, heh, heh, heh!"
   - If the children are in costume, the instructor might say, "Boys and girls, one of your favorite Halloween characters wants to say a few words to you." Present one of the Halloween puppets and have it say something like this: "Happy Halloween, boys and girls. You sure look scary! I see a pirate/ghost/witch over there. Oooo . . . . And there's a _____. (Pause) I wonder who's hiding behind that _____ mask?" Name off some of the Halloween characters the children are portraying. Example: "Ghosts, goblins, witches, _____ _____ and _____. They are all here in this room. Oooo. . . . Good-bye now. I hope you have a scary Halloween."
3. To have a Halloween character designate which students are to line up first for dismissal. For example, say "I've asked one of your favorite Halloween characters to dismiss you for recess/lunch/_____."
   - Halloween character: "Hi, boys and girls. I want to wish you all a happy Halloween.(Pause) Right now it's time for _____, so I'm going to call out who's to line up first." The Halloween character should call out groups of students by rows, tables, first initials, or whatever. After the students are all lined up, the puppet can dismiss them. "Happy Halloween. Good-bye, you may go now."
4. To make a display of students' work
   - If you have spacious bulletin boards, you may want to display a sample of each student's work (math/penmanship/whatever) next to the puppet the student made.
   - The student-made puppets, as examples of art work, might be pinned to a clothesline strung inside the classroom.

Student Use

Here are ways students may use the puppets.
1. Have each student make a Halloween puppet of his/her choice.
   - The puppets may be considered mainly a holiday art activity, if desired.
   - Ask the students who made witches to come as a group to the front of the room to show their puppets. Have them say "Happy Halloween" or sing a Halloween song together. After these students have returned to their seats, let the students who have made cats repeat the procedure. Continue until all of the Halloween characters and students have had a chance to be presented.
2. Let several students with various puppets present a skit.

Recreational Use

The puppets may be used in recreational settings, such as at camp, at home, etc.

Witch's face

Witch's body

Cat's face

Cat's body

Ghost's face

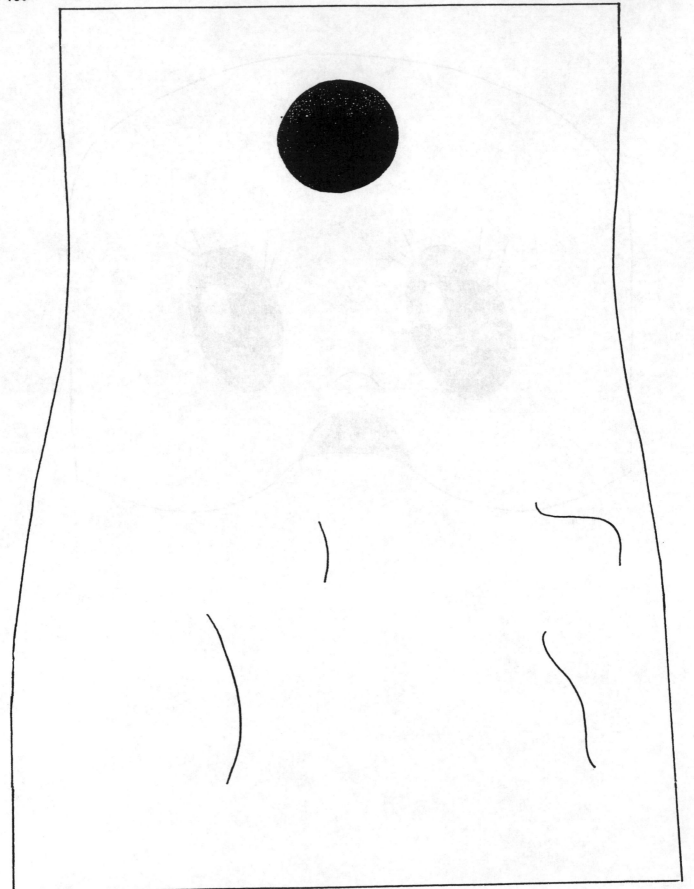

Ghost's body

Jack-o-lantern's face

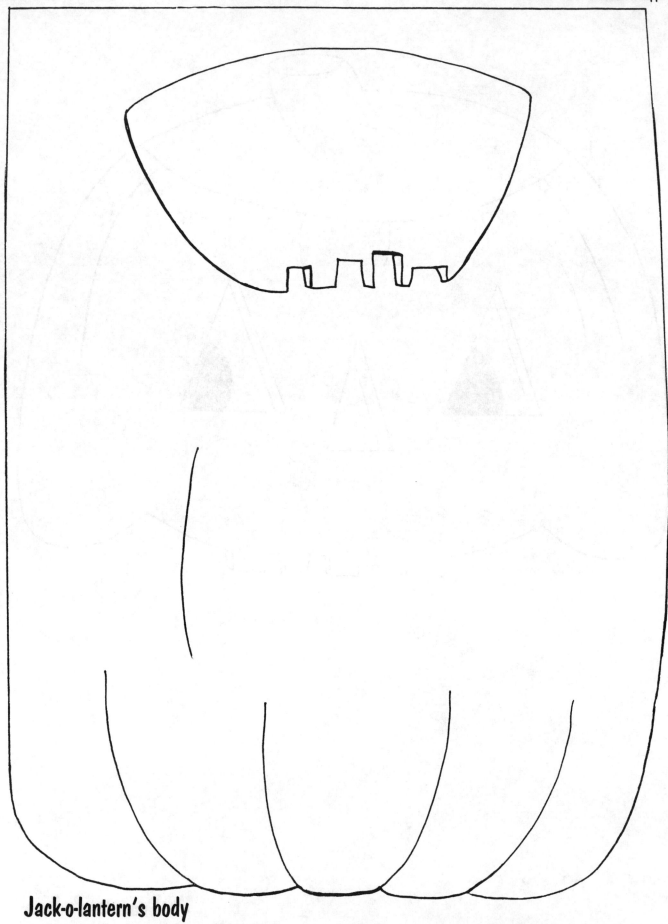

Jack-o-lantern's body

Scarecrow's face

Scarecrow's body

Bat's face

Bat's body

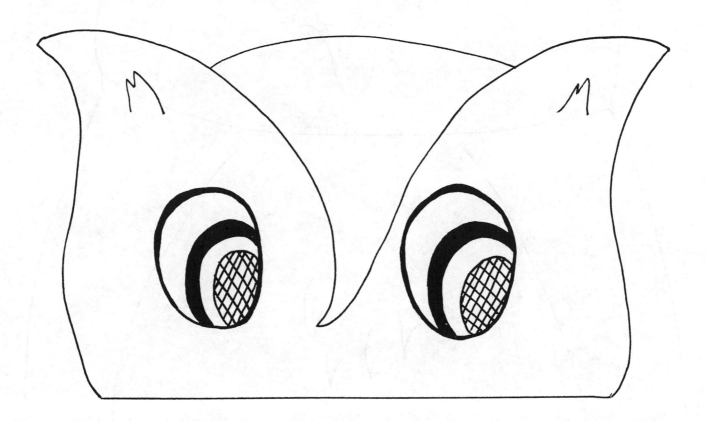

Owl's face (match chin lines of two parts)

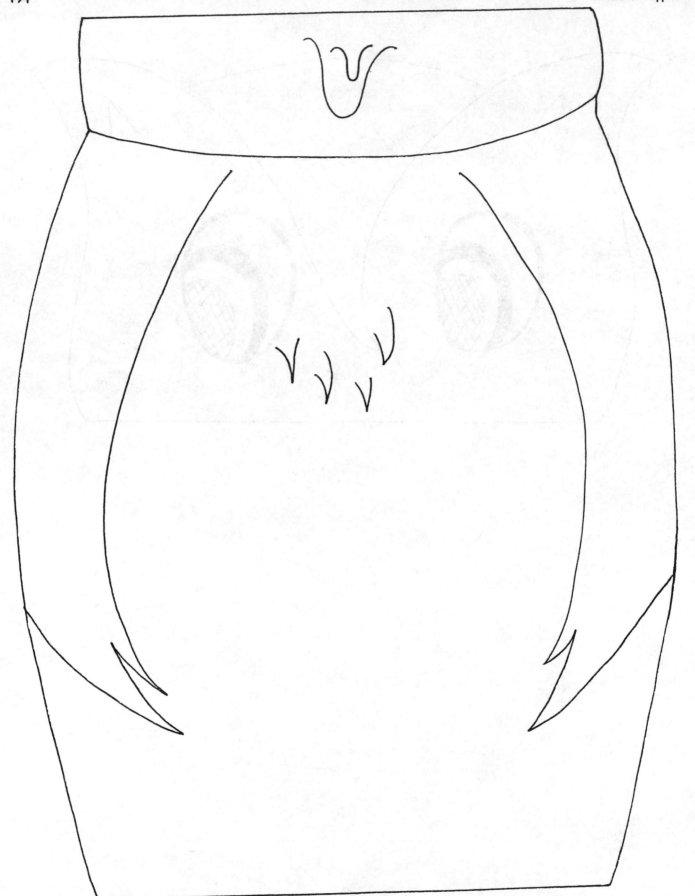

Owl's body

Finger Puppets

1. Photocopy the finger puppets on the paper of choice: typing paper, tag board, or construction paper.
2. Color the puppets, if desired.
3. Cut the puppets out.
4. Fasten the cuts in the finger bands.
5. Hold a puppet's band with the first finger and thumb.
6. Move the hand to animate a puppet.

Index

Puppets are designated by *P*, Riddles by *R*. In story listings, puppets are for the title characters unless noted otherwise in parentheses.

About the Author

Arden Druce has been a school librarian for twenty-one years, serving elementary, intermediate, junior, and senior high schools. She has also been a teacher of grades one through six. Mrs. Druce is also the author of *Complete Library Skills Activities Program: Ready-to-Use Lessons for Grades K-6; Chalk Talk Stories; Witch, Witch;* and *Library Lessons for Grades 7-9,* Revised Ed. The author lives in Camp Verde, Arizona, with her three dogs and six cats. She is currenty devoting her time to writing, studying, and animal welfare.